OIKOS

Tom Mercer

Unless otherwise noted, all Scripture quotations are from the New International Version of the Bible.

OIKOS, Your World, Delivered
ISBN Number: 9781-57087-709-4

Published by Professional Press
Chapel Hill, NC 27515-4371

Manufactured in the United States of America.

Dedicated to

Sheryl Lynn

Your love for the people around you is the daily reminder I need to act like Jesus. Your outward beauty makes everyone who finds out we're married think I must be rich. I will always be grateful to God for graciously dropping me in your *oikos*. I will always be in love with you for letting Him.

Table of Contents

Acknowledgments

To transfer passion from your heart to the printed page is no small undertaking. For me, it has been a profound lesson in ecclesiology to see how the gifts of the Spirit can dovetail together to bring a project such as this to life.

My deep gratitude goes to Dr. Bruce and Christine Wingard for their help in transforming the spoken word to the written word. Their amazing skill at making something I say translate well into something I write has been a thing of beauty.

I am also thankful and humbled to work in such a gifted laboratory of pastoral leadership. The men who have chosen to set aside career and ambition, to simply build an effective and enduring church together, are my constant encouragement and source of accountability.

Likewise, I am grateful for the support that HDC's ministry team has offered. From Tony Mercado's cover design to Matt Curtis' page layout and internal design; from Mary Grace's transcriptions to Josh Bishop's logistical support and constant nagging about excellence. Thank you all.

I also want to thank my church family, who faithfully and patiently let me drill *oikos* into their hearts each week. It is a blessing to regularly listen to the many *oikos* testimonies that make it clear you've taken it to heart.

Thanks, too, to my guys in San Diego, my mentor group, who have both let me rant about this theme and have held me accountable to finally finish this project.

When he realized whose son I was, a well-known church leader told me with no hesitation, "Your dad wrote the book on youth ministry in Southern California!" PF is a genuine ministry legend. But I am most grateful for the book both he and my mother wrote on my heart by not only leading me to Jesus, but by showing me what a life of service was supposed to look like.

But my deepest gratitude goes to the most important people in my life, the most important part of my own *oikos*—my wife, my children and my grandchildren. Thank you for giving me a great reason to get up this morning.

Introduction

ON BEING CHRISTIAN

Everything sin touches will die. Every time someone makes a bad decision and lets sin creep in, something dies. Sometimes the death is obscure, like when an opportunity to do something really significant simply wilts away. Sometimes it's more noticeable, like when a promising relationship slowly fades away. Sometimes it's downright tragic, like when someone loses hope, buys a handgun and a human life is thrown away.

We were forewarned. The wages of sin would be death. But, my goodness, that first one was catastrophic! The Bible says it killed us all. In hindsight, it would be easy to ask Adam, "What were you thinking?! After all God's done for you, why would you declare war against Him?" But he did. Adam fired one shot across His bow and it was on! Ironic as it seems, Adam's children have been desperately trying to make peace with Him ever since.

The sticking point was always the same. God never liked our terms for His surrender. That's why, when you pick up the morning paper and read what's going on around the world or even around the corner, you can see the world is still stuck in a losing battle.

You cannot outlast an eternal God or out-think an omniscient God or out-muscle an omnipotent God or outrun an omnipresent God. You just can't. You can only hope that He would show you mercy. Which brings us to why the Gospel is such incredibly good news.

Jesus ended the war on that very Good Friday. It might have seemed as if He was just hanging there on that cruel cross forgotten and alone, but that's only the way it seemed. In reality, He was completing the mission He had come to fulfill, slowly prying apart the talons of the enemy, dismantling the grip Satan had on our dead hearts and forcing him to sign for his unconditional surrender. And within a matter of days the POWs would start returning home.

Today, most of the people you pass by still have no idea that the war is over. They're still fighting, trying to either beat God outright or negotiate peace with Him on untenable terms. It's time they found out that they don't have to try anymore.

Does it bother you that your friends are still fighting a war they cannot win? That the people you love, and regularly do life with, are typically still stuck in their sin? No hope? No peace? Nothing to look forward to but more of the same? The prospect of a loved one eternally separated from God has got to bother you. If it doesn't, then maybe you should read something else. If it doesn't bother you, maybe you should go get a book on how to blame the traditional church for your problems, or one on how some politician is probably the Antichrist or one on how a rival denomination is so incredibly stupid.

But after all the hype about the church finally emerging; and after all the arguments over virtually every doctrinal disagreement are done (like that'll ever happen); and after all the conferences on reinventing everything that has ever been done in the name of Jesus, nothing will have really changed. Your friends will still be stuck in a no-win situation. Still, no hope. Still, no peace. Still, nothing to look forward to but more of the same, because, in spite of our deliberations in the name of Christ, we still will not have really done anything Christian yet.

I serve as a pastor to a group of people who call themselves High Desert Church. We live in the high desert of Southern California, about halfway between Los Angeles and Las Vegas. The people who attend HDC are extraordinary. Not because they look different than most people who claim to be Christ followers, but because most of them actually follow Christ. Not perfectly, of course, but intentionally, to be sure.

Being a Christ follower doesn't mean you're theologically right. It doesn't mean you're eternally safe. You may be both, but that's still not what it means. Jesus was both right and safe *before* the Incarnation. Being a Christ follower means you're on a mission of mercy. He had one thing in mind when He laid down those regal robes and let a virgin swaddle Him up in the hay. Only one thing. Your world delivered.

oikos *n*, extended household (Gr.)

1. the most natural and common environment for evangelism to occur
2. a group of eight to fifteen people with whom you share life most closely, **your** sphere of greatest influence
3. the people for whom God wants to prepare you to become an ideal instrument of His grace
4. a microcosm of the **world** at large, for whom God sent His Son—that all who place their faith in Christ would be **delivered** from the bondage of sin and enjoy life to the fullest

Chapter One:
THE QUESTION

I have a question asked of me nearly every time I finish speaking on *oikos*. Sometimes it comes from young ministers fresh out of seminary, excited with the prospects of reinvigorating the church. Sometimes it comes from church leaders weary of programs and overloaded with tasks already undertaken. Sometimes it's from experienced veteran pastors who have tried every program they could get their hands on to involve their church in the Great Commission. But, most often, it comes from ordinary believers who have grown up in church praying that others would somehow change the world for Christ. This book is for all of the above, everyone who would ask the question, because, however the question comes, it is always the same.

If we were playing Jeopardy it would go something like this:

"Our final categories are Evangelism and Church Growth."

"I'll take Evangelism for $600, Alex."

"Evangelism for $600. And the answer is, Yes, it can."

Your mind begins to race. "Yes, it can," you repeat to yourself. *That's it? That's all I've got to work with?!*

The audience holds its breath. The familiar music ticks off the remaining seconds. The other contestants wait with anticipation to see if you know the answer.

Finally, your eyes brighten. You have it, and you answer Alex correctly.

"The question is, 'It can't really be that simple...can it?'"

That's the question I get all the time. "But Pastor Tom, it can't really be that simple…can it?"

"Yes, it can." Evangelism and church growth really *are* as simple as you're going to read about in this book, however it would be a mistake to confuse simple with easy.

It's like when my wife, Sheryl, wanted me to help her organize the living room furniture in the house we had just moved into. We had everything we needed. It just wasn't organized into a natural arrangement and we found ourselves tripping over it regularly.

The truth is, the average church has all the pieces required for the transformation of a local community already. They're already there. However, the *oikos* model will mean a whole lot of your psychological furniture will end up being rearranged. Don't worry, you will like the outcome. You'll bruise less often! You have all the pieces; you just have to find the most natural places for them to go.

OIKOS IS A NATURAL

The *oikos* model is the most natural organizational principle for the lifestyle of the Christ follower and the church. Another way to describe *oikos* is that it is organic. It is totally authentic; there is nothing artificial about it. It's not imported from someone or somewhere else. In fact, it's already working in your church, your home and your individual life. For right now I just want you to know five things that are true about an oikocentric approach to life:

It *fits* all ages and levels of maturity.

It *flows* naturally out of a Christian lifestyle.

It *facilitates* the growth of Christ's church like nothing else.

It *finances* itself.

It is *faithful* to the Bible.

Perhaps the best thing of all is that the *oikos* model is simple. *Oikos is* simplicity and that's important because the spiritual heritage of our salvation is rooted in simplicity.

The direction in the Garden of Eden was simple.

Stay away from one tree.

The cost of disobedience was simple.

Death.

The Law's lesson was simple.

We're in trouble.

The plan of redemption was (and still is) simple.

Jesus buys us back.

The price of redemption was simple.

Death.

The message of the cross is simple.

Unconditional love.

The essence of salvation is simple.

Amazing grace.

In baseball lingo those are all fastballs. No junk, nothing sneaky or complicated. Ninety miles an hour, right down the middle of the plate, straight and true. So, when it comes to His strategy for evangelism, why would God throw us a curve? As I said before, nobody would ever say Christianity is easy, but it has always been simple.

THE VERSE THAT HAUNTS ME THE MOST

It might surprise you to know of all the great verses in the Bible there is one that actually haunts me the most. The Apostle James makes the statement:

"We should not make it difficult for the Gentiles who are turning to God." (Acts 15:19)

There is a context to that statement to be sure, but the essence is clear. The Apostles were like us. Left to their own devices, they tended to make everything more difficult than it should be. The Gospel was just their latest victim.

You would expect that from the Judaizers. Kings of complexity and yet they were Christians. They prided themselves on being more "legal" than anyone, but perfectionism gets complicated. For them it evolved well beyond commitment. They became impossible to please because the Law was impossible to oblige. Nobody could ever accuse them of not trying, but at the end of the day, it was like being declared the Valedictorian of Summer School—who cares?

So, before any further damage could be done, the Apostle Paul called them out. At the first Council of the church, James and the rest of his legal team were forced to deal with what the Gospel really was. Before the day was over, they at least came to grips with what it really wasn't. And what it wasn't was difficult! James' words reflect his concern that he had been part and parcel to the unthinkable: he had made it difficult for those turning to Christ. Those words still serve as a warning to us, or should.

Like the Apostle Paul, "I fear, lest by any means…your minds should be corrupted from the simplicity that is in Christ." (2 Corinthians 11:3)

WE'VE MET THE ENEMY

Some years ago, I was invited to interview with a publishing company. Its Editor-in-Chief was (and still is) one of the kindest and godliest men I've ever known. He had happened across some of my reflections about the Scriptures. I was encouraged that he believed in me and was honored that his editors would give me some of their valuable time. I walked into the main exhibition hall of the convention center that day and, quite frankly, couldn't believe what I saw. It was the world's largest assemblage of Christian publishers, corporate Christianity at its best. This is not meant as a critical commentary, business is what it is. I met many wonderful people that day, virtually all of them reflecting a sincere desire to do Kingdom work. But, that aside, what impressed me the most was how we had all somehow been sucked into a vortex of complexity.

In what has unfortunately become the competitive and complex world of faith, we have met the enemy—and they are us! While we regularly try to reinvent the church in as many ways as our conferences and seminars can explain, the biblical strategy for changing the world remains constant. The foundation of that strategy is *oikos*. And what it lacks in creativity, it also lacks in complexity.

THREE THREADS, ONE CORD

This book is really about three concurrent threads that make up one cord. There are the stories of people whose lives have been impacted by the *oikos* model. Then there is the presentation of the *oikos* model itself, what it is and how it works. Finally, there's the story of how one pastor, who passionately wanted to motivate his flock to change their worlds for Christ, restructured his entire church and ministry into the *oikos* model. And that would be me.

Let me tell you how, for me, this whole *oikos* thing got started.

These testimonies, and all that follow, while edited for space and clarity, are personally written accounts about how people have been impacted by their *oikos* or had an impact on someone in their *oikos*.

"I was raised in a non-Christian home. When I turned 18, I immediately left home to discover what the world was like on my own, and to get away from a difficult situation. I found a roommate who, it turned out, was a Christian. After living with her for three years and developing relationships with her family, I finally began to attend church with her and accepted Christ into my heart.

A year later I met my husband, who was very involved with church and youth ministry, and a year after that we married. When I think about where I came from, and where I am now, it's a miracle! God used others to save me!!"

- Shannon

Chapter Two: A NEW PARADIGM

It was amazing! Our little youth group of four had grown to more than 300, and in just a few years. The amazing part was that it was *my* youth group. I was its youth pastor, and yet all that growth had little if anything to do with me. Those young people had simply taken a simple concept and turned their worlds upside down. They had "gotten it." In fact, they had bought the T-shirt, hat, key chain and even the flip flops…so to speak. They were real fans! A few years later, there we were, ministering to more than 300 kids. Here's how it happened.

Back in 1979 I was asked by my Senior Pastor to attend a seminar lead by Dr. Win Arn on something called *oikos*. Neither of us had ever heard of it. I was then a youth pastor at a moderately sized church. I had been hired because the youth ministry had a grand total of about four. That's right, four. It was at that particular seminar that I was introduced to the basic concept I'm going to share with you. Of course time and experience have developed and refined it, but not too much. Its genius is that it's truly simple.

That seminar lit a fire under me. Up to that point I was hesitant to introduce evangelism to the youth group at all. I remembered my own experience with "evangelism" as a student and never felt comfortable. For the first time, I felt like I could be a part of the Great Commission in a natural, authentic way. My Senior Pastor encouraged me to go for it. I felt like a youth pastor unleashed! I had "gotten it." Now if I could just get my kids to "get it."

Three years later the youth group was on the verge of outgrowing the church. Over 300 students had taken this simple idea seriously and had literally turned their community on its ear. They "got it," just as I'm hoping you will in reading this book.

While this is not a book about student ministry specifically, or any of the other typical ministry groups we see in our churches, seniors, young families, children, etc., its principles apply universally well to all groups from young kids on up. That's another part of its genius.

WHAT DID WE LEARN?

A question I am often asked in ministry is how can we get young people to come to church? Maybe a better question would be, why do they stay away from church? I would be so bold as to say that young people stay away from church for the same reason most older people stay away from church: because there is no compelling reason to go to church. People need a better reason to attend church than simply "because it's the right thing to do!" They have to see how church fits into their reason for being alive.

A local church may be tempted to see itself merely as a self-perpetuating entity, inviting Christians to attend, only for the sake of keeping the church from folding up its tent. Most older congregations want young people to come to church because they want their church to survive at least one more generation. And that's a lousy reason to have a church--just to see if we can make it survive.

People young and old need to be challenged to look beyond the preoccupations of their lives and look to change their world. Young people want that. Every young generation aspires to be worldchangers, that is, until society convinces them they can't, and the demands of day-to-day survival crush the dream. Well, guess what? That youth group--the one with four kids--discovered that they could be worldchangers, at least in their own worlds. And then they did it. And that's the point.

God wants to change the world. If we are surprised, we shouldn't be. It's all through the Bible. Even John 3:16 talks about changing the whole world, one "whoever" at a time. Unfortunately, most Christians are happy with a good sunday sermon, comfortable music and lunch with their friends afterward. They aren't interested in worldchange, much less being actual worldchangers. But comfort is not the plan that Jesus, the Head of the Church, put forward and it shouldn't be ours either.

YOU MEAN THERE IS A PLAN?

Jesus designed, taught, modeled, and gave His plan to His Church. Our task is to follow it.

The plan has been there all the time. The early church had it. The modern church has lost it. But just as that youth group found out, the *oikos* model revives it! They also found that it works as well now as it did then, and that anyone can participate! It is the heartbeat of the Lord's church and the true power behind worldchange.

Oikos is not a program. It's not an event. It's not an emphasis. It is the strategy Jesus chose to build His church. It is reflected in everything Jesus did, taught and lived.

The *oikos* model gives every believer the opportunity to be God's instrument in the most effective arena possible, their own circle of relationships. Here's how it works. God has given each of us, on average, anywhere from eight to fifteen people whom He has supernaturally and strategically placed in our relational worlds. The Greeks used one word to describe this personal world—*oikos*, or "extended household." This is the world He wants to use each of us to change, *our* individual world!

God has always utilized the family unit as the primary arena for effective evangelism. But the word "families" in the Bible refers to more than we are used to thinking about when we consider families in today's world.

Hans Walter Wolf, in his Anthology of the Old Testament, said: "A household usually contained four generations, including men, married women, unmarried daughters, slaves of both sexes, persons without citizenship and 'sojourners,' or resident foreign workers." [1]

Keeping that in mind, consider the following verses about the spiritual dynamic in the centrality of the family in God's plan.

"There, in the presence of the Lord your God, you and your families shall eat and shall rejoice in everything you have put your hand to, because the Lord your God has blessed you." (Deuteronomy 12:7)

"And there rejoice before the Lord your God, you, your sons and daughters, your menservants and maidservants, and the Levites from your towns, who have no allotment or inheritance of their own." (Deuteronomy 12:12)

In the New Testament, that extended family continues to be the focus. The Greek word, *oikos,* or household, is God's evangelistic target.

In today's world our *oikos* might include the clerk at the grocery store where we shop every week, or that person at work you talk to every day. Our *oikos* might comprise several different kinds of people with different needs, but it is the eight to fifteen people God has supernaturally and strategically placed in each of our relational worlds that He wants to demonstrate His love and grace to, through us. I have an *oikos*. You have an *oikos*, and they are not the same eight to fifteen people, but it is this world, *your world*, that He wishes to change, to bring to Himself, through you.

So, the question you might want to ask at this point is, "How effective is this *oikos* stuff versus all the programs, campaigns and evangelistic systems out there?" The numbers may shock you.

"When I was in high school I was pretty bad. There was a girl who was a grade younger than me. We shared a class together, so I was really able to observe her attitude and outlook on life. Although she never spoke about God or being a Christian I saw the Lord living in her. She was positive, always smiling and happy. I wanted what she had!

So I started reading the Bible and coming to church. I saw her again after I graduated, but sadly never got a chance to tell her how much her attitude really changed my life. I've really learned from her that it's not just preaching about love but living it that counts!"

- Susan

Chapter Three:
THE NUMBERS

WHY *OIKOS*?

Consider this. Ninety percent of the people in most churches came to Christ the same way, and it had nothing to do with a pastor's sermon, a church's program or an evangelistic crusade. More than likely, even you came to Christ this way: because of someone in *your oikos*. The overwhelming majority of conversions have historically occurred within the confines of someone's relational world. Here are the percentages of those categories of people who found Christ under different circumstances:

Special need	1-2%
Walk-in	2-3%
Ministry of a pastor	5-6%
Visitation program	1-2%
Sunday School	4-5%
Evangelistic crusade	.5%
Other church program	2-3%
Friend/relative (*oikos*)	75-90% [1]

We naturally have many more opportunities to share Christ with those people we are around the most. As a result, our faith can be demonstrated to our oikos in our daily lives, which are constantly under scrutiny, on a regular basis to those eight to fifteen people. God is absolutely sold on using your extended household, your *oikos*, as the natural arena where your testimony can be clearly communicated. We will talk more later about exactly how to determine who is in your *oikos* and what specifically to do about them.

THE ORIGINAL PLAN

After healing the demon possessed man, Jesus told him to specifically:

"Go home to your family (*oikos*) and tell them how much the Lord has done for you, and how he has had mercy on you." (Mark 5:19)

Immediately following Zacchaeus' conversion, Jesus reflected on what had just happened:

"Today salvation has come to this house (*oikos*)" (Luke 19:9)

When Jesus healed the son of a royal official:

"...he and all his household (*oikos*) believed" (John 4:53)

Jesus called Levi (Matthew) to be His disciple:

"While Jesus was having dinner [with] Levi's house (*oikos)* many tax collectors and sinners were eating with him and his disciples, for there were many who followed him." (Mark 2:15)

In Acts 10 we see the first example of a Gentile *oikos* coming to Christ. Cornelius responded to the Gospel presentation that Peter made and he and his household became believers. In reporting to the church leaders in Jerusalem, Peter reflected on what the angel had told Cornelius about Peter:

"He will bring you a message through which you and all your

household (*oikos*) will be saved." (Acts 11:14)

The story continued in Philippi with Lydia and the city jailor, both of whom responded to the Apostle Paul's challenge to place their faith in Christ. Acts 16 describes how, in both cases, an *oikos* believed and were all baptized.

Our households have always been the most natural arenas where our testimonies can be most clearly and powerfully communicated.

Jesus clearly divided people into two groups. You were either His or you were not His. There was no in-between. Likewise in our relational worlds we have two groups as well, the churched and the unchurched. This is not to say that everyone who attends church is a believer, nor is it to say that those who rarely darken the door of the church are unbelievers. In fact, if we could look into the thinking of those who are unchurched, we might be surprised.

A SURPRISING LOOK

Some months ago, I was given an article from Christianity Today entitled, "Ten Surprises About the Unchurched," by Dr. Tom Reiner.[2] Over the course of three years, his research team of seventeen men and women took to the streets of the good old U.S. of A. They covered all fifty states, interviewing a diversity of ethnic groups and socio-economic groups. Wide-ranging demographic areas were also covered, and as many females as males were interviewed. There were those from a modest education all the way to doctoral degrees. Every person interviewed was deemed to be both unchurched and non Christian. During those three years, they uncovered these ten surprises:

1. They discovered most of the unchurched would prefer to attend church on Sunday morning, if they attend at all. For years, at HDC, we believed that our Saturday evening service, which is one of the most

popular services at our church, was a service provided primarily for the unchurched. We have since discovered that Dr. Reiner is right on, at least in our neck of the woods. Most of the people who come to HDC on Saturday nights have attended church most of their lives.

2. Most of the unchurched feel guilty about not attending church. If they feel guilty, then why do they avoid church? According to the research, they discovered that the unchurched do not feel as if they can fit into the protocol of a local church. They feel they will be out of place.

3. They learned that 96% of the unchurched are at least somewhat likely to attend church *if* they are invited. 96%! Only 21% of active churchgoers ever invite *anyone* to church in the course of a year, but only 2% of active churchgoers invite an *unchurched* person to church over the course of a given year. That means of the 160 million unchurched people in the United States, *154* million of those folks would be at least somewhat likely to come to church if someone would just invite them!

4. They discovered that very few of the unchurched ever had someone share with them how to become a Christian. That is not a surprise in light of the fact that so few people invite an unchurched individual to attend church. It is not a shock to discover that neither do they invite them to know Christ.

5. They discovered that most of the unchurched have a positive view of pastors, ministers and the church. Only a few said they thought that clergy were hypocrites or only after their money. That again was a paradigm shift for me because I had been told that everybody who didn't go to church thought the only reason I wanted them to come was to tithe. And evidently, according to the research, that is not the case.

6. Many of the unchurched have a church background, which tells us that they left church for a reason. And the reason is because many of them attended churches that had no relevance to them, which

means if you're going to reach them, you may have to rethink the way you do church.

7. Some types of cold calls are effective, but many are not. The definition of a cold call is simply engaging in a conversation to which you have not been invited. One guy said, "Well, I don't mind talking to people from churches, but please don't show up at my home without an invitation. It reminds me of a telephone solicitation, only worse."

8. The unchurched would like to develop a real and sincere relationship with a Christian.

9. The attitudes of the unchurched are not correlated to where they live, their ethnic or racial background or their gender. In other words, the same attitudes tend to cross over all of those boundaries.

10. Many of the unchurched are far more concerned about the spiritual well-being of their children than they are about themselves.

Let's see now, if 96% of the unchurched population might be receptive if someone invited them to church, and if they would prefer to come on Sunday, and if most would like a sincere relationship with a Christian, and if the vast majority never had anyone tell them how to become a Christian, what are we waiting for? Sounds like *oikos* to me! I would bet that every one of those 160 million people is part of some believer's group of eight to fifteen.

WHAT'S HAPPENING?

As Harry Flugleman once said, "We strayed from the formula and we paid."[3] One of the things we've discovered over the last 150 to 200 years of church history is that we have in many ways abandoned God's plan. We have relegated His first love, redeeming all mankind "that none should perish," to some kind of optional church program, and we've paid a very dear and eternal price. We can start reversing that today, and doing that is easier and simpler than any big evangelism program you have ever tried. In fact, *oikos* is the greatest evangelism process you've never heard of. You'll see.

Naturally, there is a question that will come up about now, "What about all the big crusades where people do come to Christ?" "I got saved at a Billy Graham crusade," is a common response to the survey question "How did you come to Christ?" But you know that in those same surveys we learn that the way they even got to the arena in the first place was, are you ready? Someone in their circle of friends and relatives (their *oikos*) asked them to come and brought them. Dr. Graham knew the formula. Don't you remember, he always said, "Your friends will wait for you."

"I was at a difficult and transitional time in my life. I didn't consider myself a Christian, but I prayed daily for help. A coworker and I had become friends through a mutual love of horses. The more I got to know her, the more I noticed something in her life that was very interesting to me. I guess you could call it balance. I asked her how she did it and she said, 'I eat food for my body, go to school for my mind and go to church for my soul.' I responded by saying I ate and went to school but wasn't going to church. She asked if I wanted to go to a women's Bible study with her at her church.

It was during my first visit that I felt peace. Something happened that I can't explain, but I sensed God working in my heart that day. I know now that God had heard every one of my prayers and that He did what He needed to do to draw me to Him. I am forever thankful and blessed."

- Karen

Chapter Four:
FOCUSED ON PURPOSE

What is the purpose of your church? When I ask people to tell me what the purpose of their church is, most of them quote a verse or tell me about some noble endeavor. But, more often than not, their responses don't have anything to do with the purpose of a church.

Executing a plan requires focus and a solid knowledge of our purpose. Purpose, planning and focus are intertwined so tightly as to be inseparable. When we know our purpose solidly, then we can work our plan confidently with laser-like focus.

And while we're on the subject, you don't get to vote on the purpose for your church and neither does your leadership board. Your opinion does not matter. My opinion does not matter either. The purpose of the church was given to us by Jesus, the Head of the church. Our job is not to come up with it. Our job is to execute it.

My mission in life is to educate Christians about their reason for being alive. What we have called evangelism is, in reality, the first scene in a drama entitled "worldchange." Helping Christians discover their purpose for being alive, and then preparing them to be good at it, frames my lifework. It is a horrendous waste of our created design, not to mention of the precious time we have on this planet compared to the eternity that awaits us, if we settle for anything less than world-change.

When the truth that God put us here for a reason—to be a part of the greatest initiative in the history of mankind—burrows deep roots into the soul of a believer, and they understand that they are the only person who can fulfill that purpose in their relational world, then something transformational happens. When believers "get" that your church, my church, the whole church, exists solely, and I mean solely, to prepare you and I to better fulfill that purpose, suddenly your church becomes a much more compelling place to be. Why? Because when people live in the everyday reality of doing life with their *oikos*, going to church becomes a "want to," not a "have to." It becomes compelling.

THE GOD OF THE NICHE

Before we turn around, the Christmas season will be upon us again. I'm going to take a shot in the dark here. I don't think you're going to give the same gifts to everybody on your list, because certain gifts are appropriate for some and other gifts are appropriate for others. I don't think I'm going to give my daughters a socket wrench set, although my sons might truly appreciate one. Well, don't you suppose God is at least as discerning as we are? Neither does He give everybody in your family the same spiritual gifts or everybody in your church the same spiritual gifts. You see, what Jesus did is He niched the Body of Christ for maximum performance. He gave you certain specific spiritual abilities.

In fact, if a group of us were in a big room right now, (I actually do this when I speak on this subject) I'd have everybody in the room raise their right hand and take the spiritual gifts vow. "Repeat after me, 'I stink at most everything.' Put your hands down. You passed." God has created you and me to be horrible at most everything. The reason

He wants us to be horrible at most everything is because He wants us to focus on only a few things. He wants us to become specialists. He wants us to become very good at one thing or a very short list of some things.

What's a niche? "A niche is a position or activity, that particularly suits somebody's talents and personality, or that somebody can make his or her own." That's what a niche is. Perhaps you've heard the phrase, "You've gotta find your niche."

Believe it or not, that was precisely the strategy Jesus brought to the formation of the church. When we consider spiritual gifts, one of the great "gifts" passages is 1 Corinthians 12, where it says, "God has arranged all of the parts of the body every one of them, just as He wanted them to be." (v.18)

When it comes to evangelism, God has niched us again! He wants all of us to be involved, but with certain very specific people. And if you feel your job is to witness to everybody, then you probably won't witness to anybody. Your everyday job is not to witness to *the* world, just like your everyday job is not to exercise every spiritual gift on the list. Your everyday job is not even to necessarily look for somebody to witness to. Granted, we represent Christ to anyone we come into contact with, and some of the best times in life are those spontaneous moments when we make a spiritual difference in the life of somebody we hadn't known before. But for most of us, those moments are rare, and for good reason. Our primary responsibility is simply to be prepared to minister the grace of God to those groups of people He has already deposited in our lives. It's simple and it's genius!

At HDC our purpose is clearly stated, "To prepare every generation to change their worlds for Christ." Notice please that *their* worlds are not *the* world. "Niche thyself."

Guy Kawasaki, one of the original evangelists for MacIntosh Computers, is also a Christ follower and, in an interview for Willow Creek's Magazine, he discussed the topic of innovation in ministry.

"If you want to be effective," he said, "then you have to niche thyself. If you try to reach everyone, you'll reach no one." [1] That's true in the business environment in the Silicon Valley, and that's also true in the church.

LASER LIGHT FOCUS

Jesus told us we are the light of the world (there's that "world" thing again), so let's consider light for a moment—and not just any light but light in its most effective and powerful form—laser light. **L**ight **A**mplification by **S**timulated **E**mission of **R**adiation. A laser is a device that creates and amplifies a narrow intense beam of coherent light.

A little physics lesson now. Atoms emit radiation. Normally they radiate their light in random directions at random times and that's called *incoherent* light. That is a technical term for what we would consider to be an unorganized jumble of photons going in all different directions. Now the trick in generating *coherent* light, a single or just a few frequencies going in one precise direction, is to find the right atoms with the right internal storage mechanisms and create an environment in which they can all cooperate so that they all give up their light at the right time and in the right direction. When you can do that, the result is pretty impressive.

The power of focused light is seemingly endless in virtually every element of our lives. It has added a new dimension of efficiency in medicine, in weaponry, in electronic entertainment devices, in construction. You name it. And, oh, did I mention the church? And the difference between Christians who are coherent and Christians who are incoherent is this element of laser sharp focus. Everything and everyone cannot be a priority to us—or nothing and no one will be. If we try to evangelize everyone we will evangelize no one.

Let's laser focus on the eight to fifteen people God has strategically and supernaturally placed in our circle of influence…let's focus on our niche.

"When I was the superintendent of an inmate fire camp, several of the Fire Captains and I would meet for prayer first thing in the morning.

Our inmate clerk, who was Muslim, started asking questions about what we did and why. Most importantly, he began asking about Jesus. After several weeks, I asked him into my office to answer any questions. He accepted Christ that day."

- Tim

Chapter Five: BREAKING NEWS

Have you noticed that everything seems to be "Breaking News?" You turn on a radio station and they play their theme music and pretty soon, "Breaking News." Like every five minutes there's "Breaking News." You know, "Breaking News! The Democrats are under fire from the Republicans." That's not even news! Even the commercials are being written as though they were "Breaking News." But because the media tries to make everything important to us, nothing is important to us. It's the boy who cried, "Wolf!"

Some years ago, I read an article about a guy who went to a church conference, much like many of the ones I've participated in. During the three days of the conference, he heard this line, "The most important thing you can do for your church is…" and then the presenter offered his featured something. He heard it so often that he began writing down every occasion someone said it. At the end of the event, he realized that he heard that line 26 times in three days!

We have to know that everything can't be the most important thing for you to do at your church. There is only one *most* important thing that the church does. And, by definition, everything else *has* to be less important. That doesn't mean it's unimportant; it means it's less important.

My contention is that most churches try to do too much. And, in doing so, the most important thing gets lost in the shuffle. Jim Collins is one of this generation's most respected business analysts. He was right on when he said, "Good is the enemy of great." [1]

A few years ago I was asked to speak at a national evangelism gathering. (By the way, it was the last time that particular group asked me to come.) I made some statements about evangelism that I think were a little overwhelming for them. I said something like, "I don't understand why you guys don't just take over this whole denomination." The reason that they, like nearly every denomination, are less efficient than they should be is because they're doing too many things.

Jesus has called us to change our worlds, and we can't have time for anything else. I know that, as a pastor, the people who attend HDC could be so consumed with all of the projects we could give them, they wouldn't be passionate about anything. You simply cannot be passionate about everything.

OIKOS IS OUR PASSION

Oikos is not a program that we do at our church. In fact, at our church *oikos* is not just everything. *It is the only thing!!* And if anything that anybody comes up with at any point in time does not line up with the purpose of our church, to "prepare (individuals in) every generation to change their (relational) worlds for Christ," then we don't even consider it. It's not that we don't have programs, we do; but only if they feed into the central purpose of equipping our people to change their worlds by reaching their *oikos* more effectively.

Later on we're going to talk about how you can actually identify who's in your world. Obviously, your world is not my world, because most of the people in your world I will never meet, and that doesn't bother me. I'm thankful that God let me off the hook with your world. He knew I wouldn't have time for two worlds. I'm dealing with mine. *That* is the specific group that God has given me to target.

TARGET ACQUIRED

To a submariner there are only two kinds of vessels, submarines and targets. It's true. For the follower of Christ there are also only two types of folks, believers and non-believers. In any one *oikos* those two classifications exist as well. As it is in the macrocosm, so it is in the microcosm. Here's another way to look at your *oikos*.

Just for a moment, suppose you had the capacity to declare to everyone on the planet that you were a faithful follower of Jesus Christ, that we had the communications department of some incredible worldwide agency hook you up to speak to everyone in the entire world, translating your words into every language on earth and that, I don't know, seven or eight billion people all heard you boldly declare that you were a faithful follower of Jesus Christ. You know what? On average, only eight to fifteen people in that entire group would know if you were really telling the truth. That is your *oikos*! They are your target! They are where our primary focus should be, both as individuals and as a corporate church.

The church's purpose is to carry out the plan of God: to have the whole world come to a saving knowledge of Jesus Christ through His body, the church, one niched member at a time, one *oikos* at a time.

CHURCHED ON PURPOSE

We could also call your *oikos* your purpose because that group of people actually frames the primary reason for your breathing right now. There are many ideas floating out there regarding the purpose of church or even the purpose of a Christian life. I grew up in a ministry family, so I've probably heard all of them. There were a lot of things thrown at me, as a young man, such as why the church was in existence and what the purpose of the church was.

For many, the purpose of the church is to make sure that Christians are more and more obedient. Let's throw that one out there as a possible purpose.

MORE THAN SIN MANAGEMENT

Dallas Willard, in his book Divine Conspiracy, talks about the Christian life being relegated to what he calls, "The gospel of sin management." [2] And while sin management, as he describes it, is important, it's not an end to itself. It is simply a means to a greater end. It is something like a sports contract for a professional athlete. Some of the most successful and highly paid athletes in the world are not allowed to participate in certain activities which are considered dangerous by the general management of that particular sports franchise. They are forbidden to do some things because those things pose a risk to their contractual purpose.

For example, some players under contract are not allowed to go skydiving or motocross racing. They might not be allowed to engage in snow skiing or water sports because they're just too risky. But those athletes are not paid those incredible salaries to *not* do those things. They are paid that money so they *will* perform on the field, and throw shutouts and touchdown passes and make baskets. But in order to make sure those guys can do the do's, they are under contract to make sure they don't do the don'ts.

That is a good example of how the don'ts should operate in the Christian life. When God says, "I don't want you to do something," that's not the purpose for our life. Being obedient just makes it possible for us to do what we're under contract to do. You do realize that we too are under contract, don't you? We are not our own either. We've been "bought at a price." (1 Corinthians 6:19-20) We are under obligation to fulfill the call of the One who purchased us, who redeemed us with His blood. I mean, we are sooo under contract!

As I said, young people don't go to church because they have no good reason to go. Sin management is certainly not a compelling reason to attend church. It has never been a compelling reason to attend church. When you were a kid you didn't want go to church just to make sure you didn't mess up, and neither did I. Besides, no matter how well we manage sin, we will never manage it well enough to deserve Heaven.

"It is by grace you've been saved, through faith. It is not from yourselves. It is the gift of God, not by works, so that no one can boast." (Ephesians 2:8-9)

We are not in the church simply to make sure we become less and less sinful. Positionally, I was sinless the moment I received Christ into my life at the age of seven, when I "became the righteousness of God in Christ!" (2 Corinthians 5:21) Practically speaking, the way I see it, I will be least sinful the microsecond after I croak than I could ever hope to be in this life. I'll be with Him and there will be no sin in my life to have to manage anymore after that. But between the day I gave my heart to Christ in 1962 and that amazing day I will be in His presence, there must be something incredibly important for me to do!

Our challenge is to find that something and to make it the *main* thing in our lives. Purpose, destiny and our eternal rewards are all wrapped up in that something which is special and unique to us.

"When I was in eighth grade, I met a boy who called himself an atheist. I was starting to form my oikos around this time and he was probably the first member of it. He told me how he tried to become a Christian once, but he said he felt that God told him to back off, and that he was not welcome.

It broke my heart to see a boy my age feel as if God didn't want him, when he saw right before his eyes, my friends and I captivated by God's love. I invited him to a Bible study with my friends and me and afterward he said that he really liked it. A week later I couldn't go, but he went anyway. Later that night he called me to say, "God has come into my heart!" At that point I had been praying for this boy for three years! He seemed hopelessly angry at God, and now he has God in his life forever.

Never give up on the people in your oikos; God could use you in ways you don't even realize. I am fifteen years old; I can't wait to see how God uses me next with other members of my oikos.

- Kelsey

Chapter Six:
THE MAIN THING IN LIFE

The main thing in life is to keep the main thing the main thing. It's a constant theme at HDC, but we do have to work at it. It is so easy to get sidetracked by things that are truly important, but just not critical. Rick Warren gave us a great challenge when he said, "God's kept you here to fulfill a purpose you cannot do better in Heaven."[1] We get off task when we make those other things too "main thing" and thereby diminish the value of the true main thing. Let's talk about a few of those other things.

Everything we will mention in this chapter frames a significant component to spiritual growth and discipleship, preparing us for our all-important role as worldchangers. But, keep in mind, the church only has one real purpose. Jesus was clear on that. "That none should perish." (Let's keep the main thing the main thing, shall we?)

WORSHIP

Some people look at the purpose of the church as being wrapped up in corporate worship. All of the worship leaders at HDC know I love musical worship. They know I appreciate all they do in bringing our communities to the throne of God every weekend. But with all due respect to the worship leaders out there, the best worship in the Universe is not in your church. The best worship in the Universe is where? It's around the throne of God. If corporate worship is the purpose of the church, God might as well take us home to Heaven right now. Besides, in our carnality, we can't even worship the way we should.

"The Lord says: 'These people come near to me with their mouth and honor me with their lips, but their hearts are far from me. Their worship of me is made up only of rules taught by men.'" (Isaiah 29:3)

Have you ever been in a worship time where you knew there were going to be three fast songs, followed by three slow songs, and every song or chorus was going to be sung exactly three times? I rest my case.

When you walk into a worship service, even if you're about to hear the world's greatest worship ensemble, preparing to sing with one of the premier worship leaders in the country or are walking into the greatest worship event in the history of the church—you would still walk into that auditorium distracted by what just happened in your life driving to church. You probably had an argument with your spouse. It's a Christian tradition. Sheryl and I learned early on in our marriage, how to make sure we didn't fight on the way to church. That's right, take two cars!

My point is, often we walk into church and we're frustrated about what happened before church; we're frustrated about what's going to happen after church. You can be frustrated about the deal that didn't go down the week before; about the issue you're going to have to resolve on Monday morning; about the fact that the nursery workers didn't show up when they were supposed to and, by the time you got into the auditorium, someone had snagged your regular seat; about the fact that you thought you had on a black shirt and black pants and you realized when you showed up that it was really navy pants and a black shirt, and you look like something out of a bad Sci-Fi movie.

Then you go into worship and you notice the guy leading worship is just a little off key, or the music's a little loud, or maybe the guy in the choir, front-row, second from the left, has a really bizarre comb-over. You can't even worship without all of those things working against you. And the purpose of the church is corporate worship? It can't be. The purpose of the church can't be something that is better accomplished after the church doesn't exist anymore. What would the point be?

FELLOWSHIP

I've been in fellowship churches, where the biggest thing on the calendar is the next potluck. It's all about getting from one social event to the next. Electing officers. Lots of committees.

The problem is everybody's little fellowship group is contaminated by everybody's little quirks of style. "And if you find the perfect church," my dad used to say, "Don't join it, because the second you join it, it won't be perfect anymore."

Fellowship is often defined as several fellows in the same ship. Now don't get me wrong, I enjoy good fellowship as much as the next guy. It's just that, as the driving purpose behind having church, it won't float the boat.

KNOWLEDGE

I've been to a number of knowledge churches. In fact, I grew up learning under the ministry of some of the greatest Bible teachers in America. Even now, one of my primary spiritual gifts is helping people accumulate knowledge. But knowledge for its own sake is not the true purpose of any church.

If knowledge were the church's true purpose, then our best move would be to transform all of our churches into seminaries because that would be where worldchange was taking place. Do we see that happening? Well, not so much.

DISCIPLESHIP

Worship, fellowship and learning the Scriptures are all elements of discipleship. But none of them can really be accomplished without keeping our eye on the goal.

You may have some questions about discipleship and the role discipleship plays in the whole *oikos* concept. We have a variety of discipleship strategies at HDC, but we want our people to realize that those things are means to a greater end, they simply help us fulfill the greater purpose of the church. After listening to me rant and rave about *oikos* for an hour or so, the number one concern of Evangelical church leaders is, "But discipleship, what about discipleship?" My response is, "Disciple them to do *what*?" If Christians are not being discipled to actually be disciples, then what's the point? *"He who thinketh he leadeth, but has no one following, is only taking a walk!"* By definition, you can't be a follower of Jesus Christ unless you are actually *following* Jesus Christ. He's not just taking a walk! He organized and discipled his guys so that they could be fishers of men. And that's our job as well.

AFTER I DIE

The second after I die, I will enjoy better worship, have better fellowship and possess more knowledge about God than I ever will in this life. The same is true for you--I don't care how many theological degrees you have or are working toward. The world of academia provides a tremendous challenge and to try to learn as much as you can is a noble pursuit. It's just not the purpose of the church. God has kept you here for the time being, because he wants you to do something you cannot do in Heaven.

I may not be the sharpest tack on the board, but I'm thinking that if the purpose of the church is in any of the things we've discussed to this point, then I might not have a real good reason to stick around. If any of these things other than evangelism is the true purpose of the church, then the plan might as well be to just pray to receive Christ and then check out.

So here we are again. There truly are only two things you can do here that you can't do in Heaven—one is sin and the other is to share Christ with non-believers. Those are the two things that won't be present in Heaven—sin and non-believers. And the question is, which of those two things do you think God wants you to do while you're still here?

Once again, that is not to say the other four things we've discussed are not important. Those other elements: worship, fellowship, knowledge and discipleship are all vital to the life of a church. They all make us better prepared for our mission, so that we can more effectively fulfill our one and only purpose for being here—to provide the opportunity to know Christ for those people in our relational worlds who don't yet know Him.

At HDC we call that keeping the main thing the main thing. Star Trek fans know it by another term—The Prime Directive. Yes, we who are Christ followers have one as well.

"Sitting in the park watching the boys play soccer, I saw a mother with twin girls. I decided to walk over and talk to her. I discovered through our conversation that she and her husband were new to the area. I asked if they attended church. She said they were looking for one so I invited them to ours.

They have been close friends of ours ever since. They have been a part of our small group. A simple conversation turned into a family coming to church and getting baptized!"

- Norma

Chapter Seven: THE PRIME DIRECTIVE

The Starship Enterprise had a mission: to lead the way in exploring the vast reaches of space, "to boldly go where no man had ever gone before!" Kirk and Spock were commissioned to seek out new civilizations and bring the information they found on their voyages back to Star Fleet. However, there was a cardinal rule, a Prime Directive if you will. Under no circumstances were they to interfere with the development of a civilization.

The church also has a mission. Our challenge is not to lead where no man has ever gone, but to follow the Man Christ Jesus where He has gone, into this world, and follow according to His directives. Unlike the Enterprise, we are not tasked with reaching another world, but to reach our own; and we are not looking to bring information back, but to take the information we have, the good news of Jesus, to our world. However, we too have a Prime Directive. Whereas the crew of the Enterprise was commanded never to interfere, we are directed by the Head of the church to do exactly the opposite, to deliberately engage our worlds. The objective is worldchange. Anything less is a waste of our time on this planet.

But, in all honesty, how realistic is it for any of us to think that we could change the entire world with our little efforts, even if we worked full time at it? Not very. It isn't realistic to expect any of us to be able to affect that level of change.

So how do we fulfill the Greatest Commission ever, to go into the entire world with the good news of God's provision for the restoration of our relationship with Him through faith in Jesus?

Well, let's remember something about the day Jesus spoke those familiar words we call the Great Commission. He wasn't talking to just one man, laying the whole responsibility on one set of shoulders. He was speaking to all the disciples. He expected each of them to take a portion of the challenge, not the whole thing. That expectation hasn't changed. Obviously, we can't be responsible for changing the whole world as individuals. But we all have our own worlds that we can dramatically and effectively change. Those are the worlds which make up our individual portions. Those are worlds we can indeed change by sharing the message of salvation with them in our lifestyle, attitude, actions, example and, oh yes, sometimes even our words.

WHY WORLDCHANGE?

It shouldn't seem odd to you that I would speak in terms of worldchange. "Wait a minute, Tom, aren't we just talking about witnessing here?" Absolutely! But here's the critical point: if you define the work in terms of the tasks, what's the motivation? There isn't any. It's really just an overwhelming "to do" list. Big whoop! When someone styles their hair (not that I know from current personal experience you understand), they don't think in terms of the individual tasks involved, but rather on what the outcome will look like. It's the same in thinking about being a worldchanger. Don't think in terms of the individual tasks, but rather focus on the desired outcome—changed lives in our personal worlds. People placing a life-changing faith in Christ and then allowing him to change them from the inside out. Reconciled marriages, renewed families, destructive addictions conquered. That's a doable deal.

The *oikos* model of evangelism is authentic, organic worldchange—one person's world at a time. This is so critical that it has framed the mission of our entire church and even defined the reason for HDC's existence. Our mission statement declares we exist solely "to prepare every generation to change their worlds for Christ."

A FUNNEL, NOT A BUCKET

God began with Israel. They were the "Chosen People." The question is, what were they chosen for?

God made His commitment clear way back in the Old Testament. He was going to bring men and women from every nation back into a vital loving relationship with Himself. He chose that select group of people to be a vessel through whom He could go after the entire world! When He launched that initiative, they weren't even a group yet, they were just a guy! Abraham was the Chosen Guy.

"I will make you into a great nation and I will bless you; I will make your name great, and you will be a blessing. I will bless those who bless you, and whoever curses you I will curse; and all peoples on earth will be blessed through you." (Genesis 12:2-3)

Israel was chosen to be a funnel, not a bucket, of God's blessing. That was both a promise and a challenge. It is repeated in Genesis 18:18; chapter 22:15, 18; chapter 26:4 and chapter 28:14.

We see the literal fulfillment of that purpose in many Old Testament stories. For example, in Genesis 49:22, Jacob calls his son Joseph "... a fruitful vine, a fruitful vine near a spring, whose branches climb over a wall."

The story of Joseph details how one member of the Chosen People fulfilled his purpose—by crossing his cultural lines and blessing the Gentile world with the love of God. That purpose has not changed.

God still wants to accomplish what He began when He instituted the plan of redemption: reaching the whole world. He never intended that Israel would be grace collectors, but grace channels.

For a while, that bucket mentality of the nation of Israel continued on in the church. The same resistance to reaching out that plagued the Jews before Christ continued to plague them after they believed in Christ. By the time of Jesus' ministry, the attitude among the religious was a definite "us" against "them" mentality. Many of them only wanted to reach their own people, the Jews. However, in Acts 15, at the Jerusalem Council, the church leaders finally realized God meant what He said. He was going global with this thing and those guys better get on board.

"Therefore go and make disciples of all nations..." (Matthew 28:19)

"You will be my witnesses in Jerusalem, Judea and Samaria, and to the ends of the earth." (Acts 1:8)

James concluded as he addressed the Council: "It is my judgment, therefore, that we should not make it difficult for the Gentiles who are turning to God." (Acts 15:19) Do we "get it?" The call of the church is to connect the world with the good news of God's love. In that sense, our job is no different than the one God gave Abraham all the way back in Genesis.

Is that us? Or do our own churches suffer from the bucket mentality? Does yours? Does our disinterest in the state of hopelessness of those all around us make it difficult for our neighbors and friends to see Jesus when they look at us? Jesus came "to seek and to save what was lost." (Luke 19:10) When we make our plans for tomorrow *that* should matter. This is now our job. It's an exciting job. And we get to do it!

THE BIG PICTURE

The 5.3 billion people in the world are divided into 24,000 people groups. Of those 24,000 groups, 12,000 are "reached." These comprise cultures where a viable indigenous church movement has been established.

On the other hand, 12,000 people groups, comprising 2.2 billion individuals, do not yet have a viable church movement. These groups include 4,000 Muslim people groups, 3,000 Tribal people groups, 2,000 Hindu people groups, 1,000 Chinese people groups, 1,000 Buddhist people groups and 1,000 other people groups, all with virtually no evangelical presence.

Understanding the specific task of the individual believer is the critical theme of this book. But understanding how that task fits into that big picture of God's plan for a global Christian movement is also important. As we will see next, evangelizing the world is a process that involves three distinct steps, and God has a different method of revealing Himself in each case.

My oikos is on MySpace. Two years ago, my brother committed suicide. I started a memorial site for him. His site had fourteen friends and seven comments. Then God told me to revamp the site and really dedicate it to Him.

When the site was redone, in one month God brought 327 friends, 383 comments and it has had 3,198 views. There have also been eleven suicides thwarted from the enemy and these folks now will live eternally because of their belief in Jesus!

- Christine

Chapter Eight: DEJA VU ALL OVER AGAIN

Have you ever seen someone you recognize, you just don't know why? As Yogi Berra once said, "It's *Deja Vu* all over again!" As missiologists (those who study missions) explore unreached cultures, it becomes more and more apparent that God had arrived long before the first missionaries. Legends, oral traditions and written cultural histories will have illustrations that carry biblical principles throughout a particular culture. That's why, whenever a believer enters an unreached culture and shares Christ, they often hear, "Wait a minute, we know this Man, Jesus!" or "We understand about sin or grace." And they are right! God has laid out the groundwork ahead of time and, when the missionary connects the dots for them, they get it.

Solomon said it very eloquently; "He has made everything beautiful in its time. He has also set eternity in the hearts of men." (Ecclesiastes 3:11)

Paul was intrigued by the fact that Gentiles seemed to behave as if they were consciously conforming to the Law of Moses, even though they had never heard of it. He later came to conclude:

"When Gentiles, who do not have the law, do by nature things required by the law, they are a law for themselves, even though they do not have the law, since they show that the requirements of the law are written on their hearts, their consciences also bearing witness, and their thoughts now accusing, now even defending them." (Romans 2:14-15)

THE LESSON OF THE ATHENIANS

The situation was critical. Thousands of Athenians had already died. A plague had descended on that great city and her people were quickly losing hope. They had prayed and sacrificed to every god they knew, but none had responded. The members of the great Athenian Council were desperate; so much so, they were willing to ask anyone, even foreigners, for advice. After much debate, they agreed on a plan. Within days, an emissary was dispatched to the Island of Crete to find a man named Epimenides, a renowned philosopher, on whose wise shoulders the fate of that great city would rest.

Epimenides walked the streets of Athens, appraising the dire situation he was finally able to see first hand. He concluded that the Athenian people must have somehow offended a god they did not know existed. That god, therefore, had not yet heard their appeal for mercy. Epimenides then requested access to a large flock of sheep. He released them all early the next morning to graze. He and his aids watched closely to see if any of the sheep would lie down.

What sheep tended not to do, he believed, was rest early in the morning when they are notoriously hungry. Therefore, if any did, his logic concluded, this unknown god would be identifying which sheep He would accept as a sacrifice in lieu of His wrath. To the Athenians' surprise, several sheep actually did lie down to rest, and each one of them was slaughtered on the very spots they had rested, sacrificed on altars that were quickly built to honor this unknown God. Within days, the plague lifted.

The events I just described are not simply embedded in Greek mythology; they are part of recorded history. In fact, 800 years later, at least some of those altars were still in place. Diogenes Laertius, a third century Greek author, confirms, "Altars may be found in different parts of Attica with no name inscribed upon them, which are memorials of this atonement." [1]

Sandwiched in history between those two men is someone you're probably more familiar with. More than 500 years after Epimenides and 300 years before Laertius, the Apostle Paul found something on Athens' Mars Hill that would provide him an opportunity to explain to the Athenians a different kind of sacrifice. A student of history and well acquainted with Epimenides, Paul boldly declared in Acts 17:22-23, "Men of Athens! I see that in every way you are very religious. For as I walked around and looked carefully at your objects of worship, I even found an altar with this inscription: TO AN UNKNOWN GOD. Now what you worship as something unknown I am going to proclaim to you..."

God had planted, deep in Greek history, an explanation of who He was and then He prepared Paul to help them make the connection. On that day, Athens would learn about another Lamb whose sacrifice would appease God's wrath and save the world.

THE BRIDGE BUILDER

God had essentially set up the Greek people, and they are not alone. According to Don Richardson, whether you talk about the Jewish sacrificial system, the Dyak Tribe of Borneo or the Asmats of New Guinea, the same phenomenon exists. In his book, Eternity in Their Hearts, Richardson makes his case. "Before the Gospel arrives, no matter the indigenous culture or religion of a people group, God has already designed a prolific feature of that culture to serve as a bridge to the person and work of Jesus." [1] God has made His own introduction to unreached people groups.

By the time believers show up in an unreached culture, the emphasis is less about an introduction and more about an explanation.

One of the women from our church traveled with a missionary organization to China for a short-term mission trip. When she returned she told this story.

"We were sharing the story of Noah's Ark and how God's grace had saved all eight people of Noah's family. 'We know about that story' they said. 'How do you know about Noah?' we asked. 'Well, we didn't know his name until you told us, but in our language the Chinese character for grace is eight people in a boat.' We were blown away! He was not only with us on that trip; He had gone ahead of us."

"All authority in heaven and on earth has been given to me. Therefore go and make disciples of all nations, baptizing them in the name of the Father and of the Son and of the Holy Spirit, and teaching them to obey everything I have commanded you. And surely I will be with you always, to the very end of the age." (Matthew 28:18-20)

USED BY GOD

So then, how does God use a reached culture, such as ours, to evangelize an unreached culture? Once God has introduced Himself, He explains Himself through the corporate efforts of the established church as they reach out to a new culture. To efficiently function in that capacity, the established church needs to develop a widescreen vision, the ability to see the immediate, local evangelistic opportunities (found in *their* worlds) as well as the global evangelistic opportunities (in *the* world).

Acts 13:2-3 records that, "While they were worshipping the Lord and fasting, the Holy Spirit said, 'Set apart for me Barnabas and Saul for the work to which I have called them.' So after they had fasted and prayed, they placed their hands on them and sent them off."

A FULL-COURT PRESS
GOD'S PLAN FOR GLOBAL EVANGELISM

EVANGELISTIC ARENA	DIVINE ACTION	PROCESS USED
To unreached cultures	God Introduces Himself	Through Cultural imprint
Through a reached culture	God Explains Himself	Through Global missions efforts
Within a reached culture	God Reveals Himself	Through Oikos networks

This book is dedicated to the demonstration of God's grace within a reached culture. God doesn't just give us a job to do (evangelism). He gives us a work we will succeed in. Whether you're an ambassador of the Gospel traveling to another culture on the other side of the world, or simply walking across the street to help a friend in your world, you will eventually find a bridge that He has supernaturally and strategically placed for you to cross. It might be a mutual friend or a common experience. It could be a love for fishing or cooking or Shakespeare; gas for a lawn mower or a television set that quits working ten minutes before the biggest game of the year. It may loom as obvious as the Golden Gate or be so subtle you won't realize it was there until after you've crossed it. But God is always the engineer, every relationship's architect.

We should never swagger into our relational worlds, boldly declaring that we have arrived to save their sorry selves. We were never designed to wear arrogance very well, but we must never be shy about our mission either. Every time we open a dialogue or pull up to

Starbucks for coffee or try to figure out a way to invite someone to an Easter service, we should do so with confidence and anticipation.

Eventually, we will stumble across one of those bridges, one that God has built at some point in their past. And on the other side of that bridge you'll find that same God, already waiting—sitting right there next to that member of your *oikos* who, without even knowing it, has always been destined to finally hear about that unknown God and His unbelievable love.

"My ex-husband and I met Paul and Dawn while we were married. They would always encourage us to attend church with them. When my husband later left me, those friends stuck by me, prayed for me and took my children and me to church with them. They told me what Scriptures to read to help heal my broken heart. At that time, I had nothing, no money, no job and no place to live. They introduced me to a friend of theirs who helped me land the perfect job. God helped me through the pain by placing those very special people in my life."

- Lori

Chapter Nine:
KEEP IT SIMPLE FOR SUCCESS

We all know about the KISS principle (keep it simple, stupid), but I'd like to change that around just a bit. Let's make it stand for **K**eep **I**t **S**imple for **S**uccess.

Anyone who knows me knows that I'm a simple man. My gift as a teacher is to break down an idea into its most fundamental form, or as some have said, "To put the cookies on the bottom shelf." Maybe that's why I'm so drawn to the Bible. It's not rocket science. When someone tells me that they don't read the Bible because they can't understand it, I know they're probably not telling the truth. They probably haven't really read much of it.

Certainly, the Bible contains lofty concepts too wonderful for us to even pretend to fully understand (the price we pay for mortality), but those passages comprise only a small fraction of the Scriptures. Even the simplest among us are able to understand virtually all of it. Had God wanted to remain a mystery, He wouldn't have written the Bible at all. He wants us all to get it. He just doesn't want us to think we can improve it. He knows that if we try to make it better, we'll only make it more difficult.

The main thing that has stuck with me from Dr. Win Arn's seminar on evangelism wasn't profound really. It was just so incredibly simple. It had never been modified. From generation to generation, from culture to culture, from Testament to Testament, it was as uncomplicated as it was consistent.

Until that day I had hated the thought of witnessing. The funny thing was, up to that day, God hated the way I thought about it too! Hearing Dr. Arn sent me on a journey I have yet to complete. What he said stirred me to action. I investigated it, and it was true. I tried it, and it worked! I taught it and it changed the way people saw their world. Now I lead a church full of people who are energized by it, and I am reminded everyday that it really is *that* important, and that it really is *that* simple.

But, in order for the light to go on for me (and perhaps for you too), I had to be willing to set aside those biases that have so complicated the simple challenge of the Great Commission. In a word, a simple word, *oikos*, you can discover the key to worldchange; and when you do, you will discover something you've always wanted—your world delivered!

A UNIFIED CHURCH

One of the most exciting things about the *oikos* model of evangelism is that it is incredibly effective at unifying a church. Does your congregation have a strong sense of why, exactly, their church exists, and what its purpose is? Is that purpose a supportive fit for their life purpose?

Oikos provides that. We said early on that one of the characteristics of *oikos* was that it fit. The purpose of the Christian life and role of the church should likewise be a natural fit. If demonstrating the grace of God to their *oikos* is a passionate purpose for any believer, it follows that preparing him or her to fulfill that purpose is the reason for any church's existence. Like we said, it's not rocket science. Unfortunately, some churches have so many programs the people can't possibly stay on task.

The reason that churches and church families have conflict is because they're off task. If I have time to be critical of you, then I am not focused on the reason God has put me here. I'm drawn to the passage in 1 Corinthians chapter 1, where Paul's talking about division in the fellowship: "I'm of Paul," "I'm of Apollos," "I'm of Cephas," and then all the real spiritual guys say, "I'm of Jesus." They have all this conflict in the Corinthian church. Then, a few verses later, the Apostle says, in effect, "You all better clean that up or the cross of Christ will be emptied of its power."

Stop and think about the strength of something that can suck the power right out of the cross. That's something. And that something is division in a church. God can use a lot of different kinds of churches—different sizes, different styles, different doctrinal bents. He just can't use a church where the people are fighting each other instead of the enemy. When I talk to leadership in churches where there's this divided loyalty going on, all I can say is, "You all better clean that up or your mission is over." The power of the cross is, to a significant degree, vested in the unity of those who bear the message of the cross.

A DIVERSE GROUP

So what do you do when you have all these people of different religious and cultural backgrounds? First, you realize that they are there. In the membership process at HDC, I go through a little exercise. "Ok," I say, "How many of you come from an Assembly of God background?" A bunch of people raise their hands. "Calvary Chapel?" another group raises their hands. Through the list I go, "Methodist, Presbyterian, Church of Christ, Baptist? What about Catholic? Or how about a Mennonite or two?" We've got some of those, too.

Secondly, you understand, accept and realize (yes, all of that or it won't work) that they will NEVER be united on the basis of your or anyone else's doctrine. It's a fact! In fact, the larger a church becomes and the more doctrinal passions are present, the less potential there is for unity, unless there is a compelling and even overwhelmingly greater purpose for that church to meet together.

You know as well as I do, if you want to start a range war in your church just get into a diverse group and start talking doctrine. Don't believe me? Just throw a few sensitive theological ideas on the floor and watch them devour each other. In fact, I'm so bold as to say I can get a group who comes in shaking hands and hugging and everybody looking at name tags, everybody drinking coffee and eating donuts, and I can have them at each other's throats in about ten minutes.

If I raise certain doctrinal subjects, or certain theological ideas or church policy issues, at some point their blood pressure is going to sail upward and they're going to become very defensive. The group will separate into factions and we will not be one bit closer to changing our worlds for Christ. In fact, we'll be further away after we met than we were before we came. Futile? Definitely!

In a healthy church, one driven by the right purpose, discussions, even difficult ones, about controversial doctrines are not only possible, they're encouraged. But only because we can end those discussions with, "Isn't it great that agreeing on this matter isn't essential to our real reason for meeting together?" I would never suggest that Orthodox theology is not important. But since you'd be hard pressed to find two people who have exactly the same view of orthodoxy, I'm just suggesting that you give them something more important to do than argue!

Like a ship with many different sails, if we don't all work in unity we can't accomplish anything. Not only that, even if we get all the sails set the same way but there is no wind, guess what? We still go nowhere. Just like a ship's sails have to be set properly and there must be a wind to give the ship steerage way, so too must a church have a common purpose among its people and its leadership, and the wind of the Holy Spirit to energize that *one* purpose!

JOB SECURITY

For people in my vocation, job security often means just keeping a church together. So how can we hope to do that when we have such diverse congregations? In fact, you might be proud to say, "My church is not diverse." Well, if that's the case, then you're not reaching out to your community because your community is very diverse. In fact, if people are coming into your church and they are finding Christ, then your church is actually becoming more diverse every single day. And, eventually, it's going to catch up with you! How are you going to keep that together? You have to keep them and yourself on task. Don't give them time to think about how wrong everybody else in the church might be.

You see, *oikos* is the main thing, because it is our purpose. When believers figure that out, it becomes the great equalizer in any church. I don't care how good looking you are or how unattractive you might be. I don't care how tall you are or how short you are. I don't care if you have money. I don't care if you're flat broke. I don't care about your ethnic background. I don't care about your theological background. Actually, I don't care about anything except that I just know you've got eight to fifteen people that God has supernaturally and strategically placed in your sphere of influence, and you've got a job to do today. That job is to communicate to them the amazing grace of God. When you and your people catch that vision, they don't have time to bicker and fight. It eliminates petty theological hair spitting.

WHAT WE DO

I have people say, "You have thousands of people at your church. How do you keep all those diverse folks all looking in the same direction?" By constantly reminding them of their purpose! Some of you reading this book have been in our church and you know this is true. Every single week, in virtually every single service, I'll say something to this effect, "God has brought eight to fifteen people into your sphere of influence. He has surrounded you with this group of individuals, strategically and supernaturally, because He wants to reach out to them and He wants to use you in the process." And then I'll continue, "And the Greeks called this group an...," and thousands of people will say in unison, "*OIKOS*," because they know why they're there.

They're at our church because they're becoming better prepared to do the only thing that's worth staying alive for. The laser sharp focus of this *oikos* strategy is what Jesus implemented from the very beginning. It has always been His main thing. God has given all of us that one main thing. And the main thing in life is to keep the main thing the main thing.

Let's **K**eep **I**t **S**imple for **S**uccess. Now, that's a holy kiss!

I was asked to come to church by a friend six years ago, when I was going through a divorce. I started attending the young adult service on Sunday nights and I accepted Christ into my heart about three months later.

I have since met and married my husband through friends here at church, and church has become a big part of our lives.

- Joanna

Chapter Ten: IT'S WHO WE ARE

Toward the end of his long and distinguished career in comedy, Milton Berle gave much of his time to performing for senior citizens at rest homes. "As long as I'm performing here, I'm not living here," he would say. One day, a dear elderly lady sat through one of his performances somewhat aloof. Afterward, he approached her and asked her, "Excuse me ma'am, but do you know who I am?" She responded gently, "No, but if you go up to that desk over there and ask them, they will tell you."

Throughout church history, the great deceiver has waged a relentless, highly organized media campaign with one purpose in mind—to keep us believers from understanding who we really are in Christ or what it means to have a relationship with God through Jesus Christ. The funny thing is that he's accomplished it all in a very unlikely place, the Christian church.

For almost two millennia, Satan has perverted the Christian psyche into believing that the church is comprised of two groups, the haves and the have-nots; the stars and the rest of us groupies; the ones who are marching to glory and the rest of us who are crawling to glory; the ones who deserve to be favored and the rest of us who, quite frankly, are lucky to just be alive; the saints and the rest of us "ain'ts."

SAY IT AIN'T SO, JOE

A popular TV show called "Pros vs. Joes" featured good to very good amateur athletes competing against top notch pro athletes. The result was about what you'd expect. A slaughter. No comparison. Only once in a great while did the "Joe" beat the Pro in any of the contests. The training, conditioning, coaching and experience of the Pros make them virtually unbeatable. Hmmm, is there a lesson here for us? Let's see.

In the Roman Catholic Church a highly admired "servant of God" may eventually be declared a saint. Such persons are then *canonized,* or added to the "canon" or catalog of saints. Their names are invoked at the celebration of the Mass. They are the heroes, the miracle workers. They are infallibly declared by the Pope to be the beautiful people of the church. Because of their great merit, they're even allowed to intercede for the rest of us lowly, average, everyday, run-of-the-mill Christians, who vainly try to gain an audience with God on our own. It ain't so, Joe.

In Protestant circles, those who have achieved a measure of prominence are thought to be the "stars" of faith. The high-octane performers who, because of their latest accomplishment, are given the red carpet treatment, while the rest of us underachievers just have to muddle along. It ain't so, Joe.

Even in your typical Evangelical church, you'll find a similar delineation. Many will shake their heads in sympathy for their "disillusioned" Roman Catholic friends while they shake their fingers in the faces of their "over-emotional" Pentecostal brethren. And then they will turn around and distribute their own lists of fundamental requirements for God's favor, including the avoidance of certain types of wardrobe styles, cinematic indulgences and, "Lord, have mercy," even utilizing percussion instruments in worship services. All the while they are priding themselves as God's favored few while hoping the rest of the church can someday catch on. It ain't so, Joe.

YOUR BIGGEST FAN

Yes, we *have* met the enemy, and they really *are* us. All of us. We have fallen prey to the deception of the evil one. Having split Christ's body into the few who have "arrived," from the masses who simply try to survive, the deceiver has reduced the self-esteem of the average "Joe" believer to the point where he or she wonders if there is any hope of ever capturing the elusive butterflies of victory, success and joy. We long for sainthood, but are convinced it is out of reach for us. We might as well get used to it; we will always be playing catch-up. Little engines that can't, right? One last time, all together now… "It ain't so, Joe."

Satan paints a pretty bleak picture for us if we want to buy it. I don't. I suppose it depends on who you believe—your biggest enemy or your biggest fan; a lying father or a loving Father; someone who hopes to destroy you or someone who has already died for you so you could live in Him, die for Him and spend eternity with Him! Is that a tough choice? Didn't think so.

FOR THE RECORD

For the record, in the New Testament God calls the believer a "saint" sixty-two times. It's true. We are all the *hagioi,* the "set apart ones," the "righteous ones." In Paul's opening remarks to the church at Corinth, he does not address two classes of Christians. He calls all of the believers there "saints." That's right, the struggling church in Corinth was full of divisive, accusatory, immoral *saints.* But saints, nonetheless. Now, if God says you're on the list, then you're on the list, regardless of what the Pope says.

Every believer, not just a select few, is a "set apart one," positionally righteous, fully equipped, high-powered spiritual machine! That is who you are! And it's been that way from the first moment you said yes to Jesus Christ. There is no spiritual superstar on any media network, at any church, in any pulpit anywhere who has more spiritual potential than you do at this very moment. We are all the "haves." In Christ, there are no "have-nots." We're ALL saints. At some point, this has to land in our hearts. In Christ there are no "ain'ts!"

YOUR "TALENTS"

Remember, God doesn't compare us to each other. Even as human parents, we're warned about comparing one of our children to another or trying to get the one to be more like the other. Never forget the five-talent servant got the same reward as the ten-talent servant. They, as well as us, are judged according to what's been given to us to do and use. And this much can be said of every one of us. We all have eight to fifteen people that God has strategically and supernaturally placed in our sphere of influence so that He can use us to show them how very much He loves them. Accountability begins there.

Can we think of them as our field to sow in? Can we think of our lives and the moments of encounter with them as our "talents?" Your life and your time are your talents. There is an abundant life out there. It's for you. There are unbelievable opportunities out there. They're yours. Not the pastor's, not the next person's, yours. Believe it. This is the first step on the road to revival. By the way, that's *your* revival. Maybe you've never even been "vived" yet, let alone revived. Regardless, we've got to start someplace, and you're the best place I can think of.

About two weeks into High School, I was in a car crash. I was hospitalized for about four months. God saved my life and supported my family through my oikos, who were there for my family and me, and I thank God for that every day. I gave my life to Christ two years later, and it feels great. I love it!

- David

My father passed away five weeks ago. Throughout his life, he didn't want anything to do with God. But through a series of events, his heart was softened and he finally agreed to come to church. Through the church services, he finally gave his life to God. That has given my family the peace they needed to get through this tough time. We know that we will get to spend eternity with him. Thanks for the challenge. It saved my Dad's life!

- Brandi

CHAPTER ELEVEN: YOUR FIELD OF DREAMS

Who among us, as believers in Christ, have not dreamed of accomplishing something of significance for Jesus? Fame and recognition may fuel the ego, but significance is what counts. I can tell you from experience that being prominent isn't all it appears to be. One of our couples at HDC had their own Christian television show for two and a half years on a major Christian network, and they have shared with me how, at times, they felt like they had no private life. Think of it this way. My bald head is prominent, but my liver is significant. The difference is critical.

When we set ourselves to be significant in the Kingdom of God, we have to look no further than our own *oikos* to succeed. That's where we've been planted, and where God expects us to bloom…at least initially. More opportunities may indeed come, or all our significance may result from what we do in the field of our eight to fifteen. You are truly God's doorway into the hearts and lives of those people. Your *oikos* is truly your field of dreams. Besides, the smaller the field, the easier it is to hit a home run.

WHAT'S MY JOB?

So, Pastor Tom, "We get saved and then God gives us a job to do?" No, He owns us (we were bought with a price, remember?) and what He wants is for us to simply *be* His witnesses. It's not a job description, it's an identity transformation!

What we don't realize sometimes is that we are witnessing for Him all the time. Every encounter, every word spoken, every action taken is a direct demonstration of His presence in our lives. We can't help it. Our *oikos* will make assumptions and draw their own conclusions. At times, they won't be able to avoid drawing the wrong ones. But light is what it is. As we remain intentional in our role, good things will happen.

We shouldn't be surprised; we sang it years ago in Sunday School. Remember? "This little light of mine, I'm gonna let it shine."

THE GREATEST POSSIBLE IMPACT

A man once counseled his son that if he wanted to live a long life, the secret was to sprinkle a little gunpowder on his cornflakes every morning. The son did this religiously, and he lived to the ripe old age of 93. When he died, he left 14 children, 28 grandchildren, 35 great-grandchildren, and a 15-foot hole in the wall of the crematorium. That's impact! People want to make an impact, but they just don't know how.

Our households continue to be the natural arenas where our testimonies can be clearly communicated. But, why is that?

Because your life lived out in front of your *oikos* demonstrates your faith…whether you want it to or not, whether you think it does or not.

We naturally have many more opportunities to share with those people we are with most often. As a result, the faith which is demonstrated in our daily lives, is more regularly scrutinized in an *oikos*. That's why the overwhelming majority of significant conversions have historically occurred in the confines of that extended family.

THREE KEYS

There are three keys to understanding why your witness within your *oikos* is so effective.

Key 1--Your life sparks the interest of your *oikos*.

The question of what to *do* as a Christian has always been overshadowed by who you *are*. While evangelistic technique is a helpful study, the best way to prepare for effective evangelism is to simply mature in your faith.

"But in your hearts set apart Christ as Lord. Always be prepared to give an answer to everyone who asks you to give the reason for the hope that you have." (1 Peter 3:15a)

The sequence is pretty simple: Your growth leads to their interest, which leads to their questions, which lead to your answers.

Key 2--Your life silences the criticism of your *oikos*.

One of the most frustrating things Christians have to contend with is the criticism of ignorant people. Public perception of the corporate church is regularly manipulated by the media and, as unfair or unfortunate as that may be, most of the time there is little we can do about it. But the arena in which we find our greatest degree of influence is that unique circle of relationships. And the most effective way to deal with criticism is to show them who's right! Use words when appropriate, but never underestimate the clarity that comes from a faithful life.

"But do this with gentleness and respect, keeping a clear conscience, so that those who speak maliciously against your good behavior in Christ may be ashamed of their slander." (1 Peter 3:15b-16)

Key 3--Your life establishes the validity of your message.

A Ford salesman who tells you to come by and see him because the greatest vehicle in the world is made by Ford, and then waves as he drives away in a Toyota will probably not get your business. Neither will someone who preaches about God but lives like the Devil.

Aristotle said: "Persuasion is achieved by the speaker's personal character when the speech is so spoken as to make us think him credible. We believe good men more readily than others: This is true generally whatever the question is, and absolutely true where exact certainty is impossible and opinions are divided...his character may almost be called the most effective means of persuasion he possesses." [1]

EASY ASSIMILATION

Another reason *oikos* evangelism is so effective is…because new believers are more easily assimilated into the life of a church. It is a fact. They already have family and/or good friends who are involved before they get there. They naturally feel at home as soon as they arrive!

We've all heard the TV ads shouting, "Bonus, bonus, bonus. But wait, there's more!" Well, the bonus here is when people come to faith because of someone in their *oikos*, they are much more likely to take the same good news to the other members of *their oikos*. The *oikos* model of evangelism is self-replicating! It's non-threatening and duplicable. It's not too much for the new believer to understand because they have just experienced how it works. It feels natural to them. That's why opening effective channels of communication for Christ begins at home.

"But, Pastor Tom, what if my family is already saved? Then who's my *oikos*?"

Ahhh, that's next.

My uncle became a Christian while he was in jail. After my grandpa passed away, my uncle got my grandma into church and she is the one who brought me to Christ.

- Riley

My son started coming to church and invited me to come, and I've been coming ever since. I thank God that my son invited me here.

- Cindy

I worked with a church member for about five years. Her peaceful and graceful way of getting through things was attractive, and I knew it was a result of her faith. Because of her, I came to church. Then, while I was attending the single adult group, I met one of the pastors who prayed with me to accept the Lord.

- Renee

Chapter Twelve: YOUR DANCE CARD

Before my time, there was a custom in polite society which has now passed out of fashion. When at a dance, each lady would have what was called a "Dance Card." When a gentleman would ask her for a dance, she would write his name on her dance card so she would know who her partner would be for each dance.

Those Dance Cards became cherished treasures, precious souvenirs that went into scrapbooks and memorabilia boxes.

That custom seems almost silly in the Facebook and MySpace culture we live in today, but those were more refined times. Society back then had more norms and rules than it does now. People were expected to interact with their friends, neighbors and families according to certain customs.

In our culture, the amount of contact we have with these same groups is quite a bit less and more superficial. Years ago, one would always acknowledge another person as you walked by them, even if you didn't know them. But today, it has become odd when someone does. We build walls around our homes and don't get out of the car until we close the garage door behind us. We have become a society of isolated people. Most social networking occurs behind the veil of a computer screen.

Yet, there *are* still those eight to fifteen people with whom we do life; those folks with whom we regularly come into contact. They could be relatives, friends, neighbors, schoolmates, co-workers, or others we encounter on a regular basis. These are the people who belong on our "Dance Cards," if you will.

Believe me, people are generally more needy and lonely than ever. Some folks will be easy to share with, and others will find it tough getting over their wall of self-isolation, but realize that it's only their own fear keeping them behind it. People have never been hungrier for relationships or more afraid of them.

OVERCOMING THE WALL

Do the unexpected. One of our members told me about rolling a trash can back up the driveway for his elderly neighbor because he knew it was a bit of a struggle for her. She didn't know he was doing that for several weeks, and then, one day, she finally saw it was him. That led to a conversation.

Be yourself. You don't have to act like some street evangelist. Just be who you are. Your personality works the best for you, so don't adopt someone else's. You don't have to know all the answers; you just have to authentically care, and not be afraid to let it show.

Be nice. Sometimes folks get so scuffed up by the world they have to live in, all it takes is someone being nice to them to get their attention. Being nice is more powerful than you might imagine.

Be consistent. I'm going to give you five things in the next section that you can do for your *oikos*. Do them consistently and you will be stunned at how the Lord will use you to demonstrate His love to your *oikos*. After all, He's the One who placed them in your life.

Be persistent. Just because someone says no the first time you ask them to come to church with you doesn't mean they won't ever say yes. If the Lord knows He can count on you to be gently persistent, then He can set things up so one time when you ask them you'll hear, "Yes, I think I'd like that." It's happened more times than I can count.

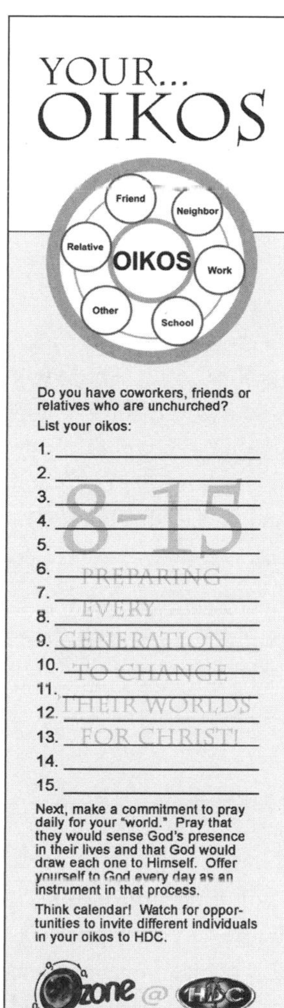

Oh, one more—listen to the voice of the Holy Spirit. This is very important. As you move into this oikocenteric lifestyle you will find more and more that you're hearing that small whisper guiding you. Listen to Him.

Throughout this book you've read short testimonies about how God used regular people to bring members of their *oikos* to Himself. Most of them didn't do big things and, whatever they did, they did for or with people they already knew. How hard is that? It may seem uncomfortable at first, but you know what? After a while it becomes a very engaging and natural lifestyle.

HOW TO USE YOUR DANCE CARD

1. Make a list.

I know that seems a bit elementary, but it is the first key step in being effective within your *oikos*. It's sort of like the old Irish recipe for rabbit stew. "First, catch the rabbit." If you don't know who is in your *oikos*, you won't follow through with the other three steps very effectively. It's not just you, it's human nature. Don't fight it.

You might want to group the folks on your list by categories such as family, work, school, etc. You'll also find that different spiritual categories are represented. Some are non-believers. They need Christ. Some are believers who have allowed other important challenges of life to crowd out the most important- preparing to be worldchangers. They need to be re-energized for a purpose-driven mission. Some are believers already focused on becoming better prepared to reach out to their own *oikos* for Christ. They need to stay the course. The point is, know your world.

2. Keep it current.

You'll be surprised at how fluid your *oikos* will become. There will be some who never leave your list, and others who come and go, and still others who will lead you to even more others. Your *oikos* will grow. Don't worry if you only start out with five or so. The Lord will bring people to your mind that should be included and release you from some as He wills. Keeping your *oikos* list current will keep you both aware of and focused on your mission. Your *oikos* list is also a great reminder of your world's fluidity. Those windows of opportunity do not remain open forever. People move away. People change jobs. People die.

3. Pray everyday for your entire *oikos*.

Oh paleease! Too simple for you? Well, God kind of likes it. It gives Him a lot to work with. Your awareness of their lives and situations will increase if you're praying for your *oikos* everyday. Your usefulness will increase. Your availability will increase because your attitude will change. You will begin to see those people the way God sees them, as loved by Him and needing Him desperately.

I suggest that you not only pray for their needs, but also pray for opportunities to share with them. Notice, I didn't say share the Gospel with them. You may well have the opportunity to do that (after all, ultimately, that is the point), but often it is just the fact that someone they know truly cares about them, or knows they are praying for them, that will open them up to the possibility of hearing the Gospel or taking steps of spiritual growth with a ready heart.

Praying for your *oikos* is the most powerful, spiritual and practical thing you can do for them! Try it, you'll see.

4. Invite them to church regularly.

Notice the word *invite*. It should be a gracious invitation, not a nag because they haven't been going. Also, it should be regularly. Who knows when you might catch them at a point in life where their need is larger than their fear? You just never know.

5. Be accountable to others for numbers 1 through 4.

Christianity is a team sport. Being part of a small accountability group will help to keep you on task. When you start praying for your *oikos* networks as a group, you'll discover that several of your *oikos* cards have some of the same entries. That's when things really get interesting, as two or more people intentionally prepare to reach out to the same individual or family.

THE CHURCH'S ROLE

In an *oikos*-driven church the major purpose for social activities is to serve as opportunities to bring members of your *oikos* to the church under less intimidating circumstances. We have an annual men's BBQ event and, each year, I fully expect a large portion of the guys to be first timers from our men's *oikos* networks. We have a clean comedy night once a year with the same purpose—invite your *oikos*. In fact, we encourage our people to buy more tickets than they have immediate family members just so they will be motivated to invite members of their *oikos*.

Our "Summer Blast" welcomes tons of kids every year, and many of them were invited by other kids. Because every child has eight to fifteen children whom God has supernaturally and strategically placed in their worlds too. Even the regular worship services are deliberately structured to attract and minister to people brought there by their *oikos*.

The church is not only a place to train believers to live their lives on purpose; it becomes a partner in the actual process of evangelism. A church who finds its groove, operating naturally and comfortably according to the model laid out by our Founder, Jesus, is a very rare but beautiful thing.

By encouraging our people to be who and what they are, there has been an organic development beyond our early hopes…and it continues at every level of ministry.

"I had a little trouble filling out my oikos card when I first received it. There were these little blank slots on the back of the card where I could write the names of people I dealt with regularly. They had category titles above them—family, school, work. Pastor Kev explained that these prayers would be the first step toward creating a deeper connection and caring between me and those people. I gave it some thought and penciled in a few names...the nephew who wanted to talk about God at a recent family gathering...the coworker who, out of the blue, recently asked me if I believed...my wife who had been having a minor but annoying health problem.

But the stupid card had yet more slots and more categories—church, neighborhood, extra curricular, other. Extra curricular? Other? What does this little card want from me, blood? I penciled in a few more names...the Christian brother who had drifted away from faith...the neighbor who gently, but persistently, mocked my church-going ways and his wife who had chronic pain. I filled in as many slots as I could and I started to pray for those people.

Kev had cautioned us not to let this become a guilt thing, not to worry if we missed a day. He said that no one was keeping score and, for a while, it would be hit and miss. Some days they would completely slip my mind. Other days, I'd tack their concerns onto the end of my daily prayers.

Then I noticed something began to happen to me. The process reversed itself...changed up. I'd think of one of these people and their problems or their needs during the course of a day and that would prompt me to stop for a moment and pray for them specifically. I wasn't just giving someone else a little space in my prayer time, I was devoting extra time outside of my normal prayer schedule to pray specifically for them. And what's more, I began to care more about these people, to take an active interest in their lives. I even began to expect my prayers to get results.

I thought some more about this weird oikos concept and came up with a few metaphors of my own. It occurred to me that God designed the Gospel to spread like a virus in an international airport…from one person to two more to four more to dozens more… and then those dozens all get on planes and take it with them to their home countries. The love of Christ propagates the way zombies do in a scary move, I thought, by contact. Salvation spreads like a juicy rumor from person to person to people around the world. So, with this love-as-a-virus idea in my head, I continued to add people to my oikos list…my sister who needed Christ, and a job…my brother who wasn't saved…a friend at church who had a non-life threatening but chronic and sometimes painful disease.

I added a friend from an internet message board I frequent who practices what he calls 'Christian mysticism,' then realized that if I added him I'd better also add the guy from the same board I don't much care for because he makes me mad.

So, frankly, this whole oikos thing is getting out of hand. It's a nice idea, but it's snowballing on me!"

- Dale

Chapter Thirteen:
THE ESSENCE OF EVANGELISM

OUR ROLE

God has never expected us to cram His Truth down anyone's throats. We are simply His mouthpiece as He works in the hearts of others, creating in them the desire to ask the right questions. We are simply the witnesses.

I grew up watching *Perry Mason*, the original courtroom drama. Perry didn't always win but, in the end, it seemed he always managed to vindicate the innocent and expose the guilty. Later came *Matlock*, *LA Law* and *The Practice*. And, now, channel surfers have entire television networks dedicated to the work that goes on in the courtroom—always dramatic, lives hanging in the balance, mystery, controversy and, hopefully, justice.

The Bible is full of that kind of stuff. It is, essentially, a divine deposition. In the Old Testament, the Law takes center stage—the first five Books of the Old Testament are referred to as the Books of the Law. The historical record that follows reads like a rap sheet. The prophets speak of certain judgment. In the New Testament, Jesus pays for our capital crimes and delivers us from the eventual verdict of eternal death.

Visualize that courtroom with me.

God would certainly sit behind the bench. He is referred to as the Source of justice, the Judge of the living and the dead.

In the defendant's seat, we would find Jesus. He is on trial. He made claims so sensational that His enemies were bound and determined to execute Him. And that's the question all of us must eventually face. Was He telling the truth or was He a con, guilty of perpetuating the greatest fraud in human history?

On the other side of the aisle, we find Satan. He is the prosecutor. In fact, the word, "Devil," comes from the Greek, *diablos*, which means accuser, or slanderer.

The Holy Spirit, on the other hand, is the chief Defender of the Accused. But while He fights for the honor of His Client, those who are left to render a verdict are feeling a bit guilty themselves.

Sitting along the wall, we find the jury, or as we have come to know them, our *oikos*. While they try to understand who is telling the truth and who is lying, the simple presence of holiness in the courtroom has placed *them* on the defensive. At some point, as their decision about Jesus is rendered, and as they finally come to grips with who He is, it will be up to each of them to admit their own guilt. That's the kind of bombshell that every season finale is looking for… at that culminating moment, all eyes are on the bench, the Accused is declared innocent, and the *jury* is exposed as the guilty ones!

Which brings us to the only chair left—the one in which the witness sits, the one you and I presently occupy. We used to be members of the jury, but that was before we became believers. Now, we occupy the witness box. It's never been a witness' job to convince the jury of anything. The lawyers get paid the big bucks to do that. But that doesn't take away this all-important role of being witnesses—those who simply tell what they know about the Accused. Without the witnesses, what would be the point?

So, we are now on the spot. The Holy Spirit calls out. "I'd like to call Tom Mercer to the witness stand!" What will I say when the accuser grills me? What will I say when the Defender prompts me to respond? What kind of witness will I be for Jesus? Good? Bad? Or just plain ugly? And we can ill afford to leave the room because, eventually, the Defender will call on each one of us.

That reality should not intimidate us. Sometimes we get the impression from the prosecutor that we are responsible to convince someone that they should receive Christ. Nothing could be further from the truth. But why would Satan want us to think we have to be convincers? The fear of failure. Our fear gives him leverage. That heavy of a burden will keep us from ever getting involved in verbalizing our faith. But we don't have to be the convincers, we are merely the witnesses.

We have no choice but to be witnesses. We don't go out to *do* witnessing. That kind of terminology has led to wrong ideas about sharing our faith. It's not something we do. It's someone we *are.*

"But you will receive power when the Holy Spirit comes on you; and you will be my witnesses in Jerusalem, and in Judea and Samaria, and to the ends of the earth." (Acts 1:8)

BEING PREPARED

God will use us to testify to anything and everything that we have prepared to share. The more we understand about His Word, the better able He will be to call on us at anytime. If we only know a little, He can only use us to tell a little. *Oikos* brings new energy to the discipline of studying the Scriptures. We no longer learn the Word to simply expand our neural capacity or impress our Christian friends or mentors. We learn with a purpose, that we might describe the full counsel of God to our relational worlds.

In John 9, the blind man didn't know much, he hadn't yet had the time to learn about Jesus. But he did tell what he knew.

"Whether he (Jesus) is a sinner or not, I don't know. One thing I do know. I was blind but now I see." (John 9:25)

That was the extent of his testimony, because that was the extent of his experience with Christ. And no matter what level of doctrine you understand, you will always have the story of your experience with Christ, what He has done in *your* life. At some point it will become a powerful part of virtually every evangelistic conversation you have, so you might as well think about it now.

Many Christians have never taken the time to think through the testimony of their experience with Christ. Yours could probably be explained in a few statements. Given the chance, those few statements might evolve into a more detailed presentation. Depending on the setting, the length and specifics might vary.

But every version should include three elements. Let's take a look at them, and I encourage you to fill in the blanks in the next section. Don't worry about someone else reading it when you loan this book to a friend. Sharing yourself and what Jesus has done for you is what this is all about. Give this some thought because your story will add a sense of passion to whatever biblical truths are relevant to your *oikos*. Here are the basic three elements of a testimony. Give it a shot.

1. Your prior dissatisfaction.

What caused you to see that you had a need for Jesus Christ? Was it an event, a tragedy, a church program?

____

____

____

____

2. Your conversion experience.

Where did you actually pray to give your life to Christ? When was that? With whom did you pray?

____

____

____

____

3. The benefits of your salvation.

What one or two things do you believe are the greatest benefits of being "in Christ?"

____

____

____

____

In addition to our story, we also have two other weapons at our disposal: the powerful tool of the Word of God and the voice of the Holy Spirit living in us.

"All Scripture is God-breathed and is useful for teaching, rebuking, correcting and training in righteousness, so that the man of God may be thoroughly equipped for every good work." (2 Timothy 3:16)

And that includes evangelism!

1 Peter 3:15 calls for us to, "Always be prepared to give an answer to everyone who asks you to give the reason for the hope that you have."

You never know who will ask, you never know what they will ask, and you never know when you're talking to a dying man. But we aren't without help in this regard.

"But the Counselor, the Holy Spirit, whom the Father will send in my name, will teach you all things and will remind you of everything I have said to you." (John 14:26)

The promise that we will be given the words with which to testify presumes that we have already taken the time and made the effort to learn those things through God's Word. That's why our understanding of how those two work together is vital. With our story in place, the Word of God in our hearts, and an ear tuned to the voice of the Holy Spirit, we develop the ability to respond to the needs of those around us, regardless of the specific need. We can effectively testify to what we know. And our testimony will be powerful.

TIMING IS POWER

Testifying about the love and power of God is easy for us when all is well. In fact, testimonies of God's faithfulness are expected when everyone's healthy and all the bills are paid. Ironically enough, though, it is during those times that the world is least interested in trusting Christ. They may not even be watching.

However, turn on the faith in a time of crisis, and the world is mesmerized, dumb-founded. They cannot, for the life of them, figure out the power of contentment in times of difficulty. The impact is profound, because it takes them totally by surprise.

"Three times I pleaded with the Lord to take it (a physical infirmity, a 'messenger of Satan') away from me, but he said to me, 'My grace is sufficient for you, for my power is made perfect in weakness.' Therefore I will boast all the more gladly about my weaknesses, so that Christ's power may rest on me." (2 Corinthians 12:8-10)

While many in the church only brag about God in times of healing or prosperity, Paul bragged about God in the midst of an illness that God remained silent about, despite the Apostle's continuous prayers for deliverance.

What about you? Have you ever given God an opportunity to use you in a difficult time? What was the result?

Understand, difficulty is not something we long for by any means. It is in no way spiritual to ask for trouble. That's a perversion of faith. But difficult times will inevitably come, and when they do, do not overlook the wonderful opportunity to be used by God in such a powerful way. You're going to be sick or unemployed or up against the wall somehow for as long as God allows anyway, so you might as well take advantage of it!

To be a worldchanger in your sphere of relationships, you need to be prepared to be the agent of change when the opportunity presents itself, in the best of times as well as the worst. That's what the next chapter is all about.

"On the death of my husband and his funeral here at church, and my testimony of faith, two of my friends from Jazzercise decided that they would come to church. They decided to ask Jesus into their hearts and then took the baptism class. We all three were baptized on the same day. It was awesome!"

- Sheila

"Our neighbors, Rich and Carol, were two of our closest friends. Although they let us bring their children to church with us, they wouldn't come themselves. We prayed for them to know Christ personally and for God to use us in any way He could.

One day, my husband, Monte, took our children up to the mountains for a picnic and short hike, leaving me at home to catch up with some housework. Their short hike turned into a very long night. They got lost. Everybody didn't have cell phones back then, so I found out they were missing when a park ranger called and said they had found my car still parked in the visitor's center lot after closing. I called our youth pastor and his wife and our neighbors, Rich and Carol, and we all went up to the ranger's station.

We prayed and waited and waited and prayed. After six hours, my fears got the best of me and I broke down and cried out to God. Our youth pastor prayed that the wind would guide the search team to my family. Thirty minutes later we heard that they had been found, and that the ranger who found them had held up his finger and decided to look in whatever direction the wind blew. Rich and Carol witnessed God's amazing power that night. Within a couple of weeks, they both made the decision to follow Christ. They have been actively involved in our church ever since."

- Julie

Chapter Fourteen: AS SIMPLE AS A-B-C

Remember the "Dance Card?" Well, when people in your *oikos* see your life of faith lived out before them, they will be curious. Sometimes their internal question will be, *"What does he have that I don't have?"* Or *"How can she be so happy when things are so rotten?"* or maybe even, *"So, how do I become a Christian, anyway?"* Whatever causes them to look to you as dealing with life better than they do, it is the nature of your relationship with them that will form the bridge to their life and allow them to be so bold as to ask you that deep theological question... *"So, what's up with you?"*

Let's look again at where these people are in relationship to you. Here's the diagram to help you group them.

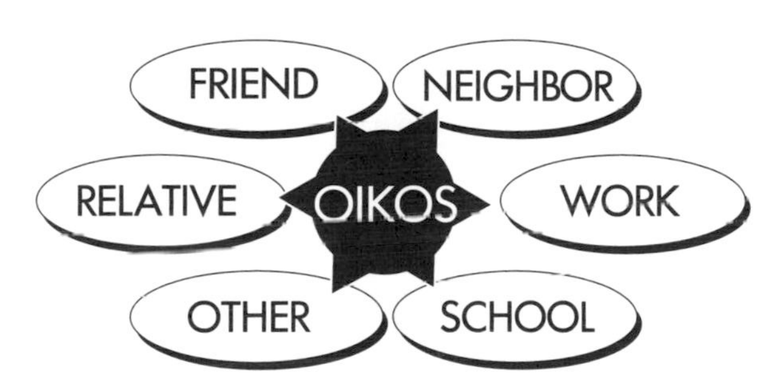

That's you in the center there…looking like a star! Now, that analogy might not be as far-fetched as you might think. You are certainly being watched. You shine brightly in their world against a dark backdrop of frustration and futility. You're a source of light for them, and finally, just like people still wish upon a star, they will sometimes look to you in desperation for help. In a seemingly impossible situation they well know that God is their only hope, and that you just might be the one He will use to illuminate the door.

So, we come now to the crux of the matter. Here is where the rubber meets the road. You're having a conversation with a member of your *oikos* and after a pause they ask you, "So, how do I become a Christian anyway?" Oh, can you feel the butterflies in your stomach struggling to get into formation? What do you say? What do you do?

A LESSON LEARNED

Back when I was in high school years ago, my dad had a hairline similar to mine. He used to say that God gave him a crew cut and the crew bailed out! (Tony Campolo's quip is the best though, "God gives every man just so many hormones- if you want to use yours to grow hair that's your problem.") Dad would grow his hair a little longer on the sides, so when he would get up in the middle of the night his Bryl-creamed hair sticking sideways made him look a little freaky walking down a shadowed hallway. That's why I'll never forget this.

He got a phone call late one night from one of our youth group sponsors, Bob Bowman, and the conversation went like this.

"Pastor Frank," Bob said urgently, "Mike wants to receive Christ." (Mike was a girl; I remember her name because she was the only girl I ever knew named Mike.)

"Well, then pray with her," dad said.

"Pastor Frank, I don't know how. You gotta come over!"

Dad sensed the urgency in his voice so he got dressed and went over there. Mike did give her heart to Christ, and dad came home and went back to bed. But the memory of being just a little bit frightened by the "killer clown" walking down the hallway has stuck with me.

Later on, I heard Bob's testimony. "After Mike received Christ and Pastor Frank had gone back home," he said, "1 fell down on my knees and in tears I told God, 'God I promise you, this will never happen again.'"

Bob was the head of the science department at our high school and was a sponsor in our youth group. Later on he became a youth pastor and, in fact, followed in my dad's footsteps at that same church. Following that, he went into missions ministry with New Tribes Mission in South America. God did a wonderful work in Bob's life, and I still remember him telling us that story with tears in his eyes.

I don't want any of the people in our church, when somebody in their *oikos* asks, "How do you become a Christian?" to say, "Well, let me call Pastor Tom." I don't have time to talk to them. Now, don't think I wouldn't find time. Of course, I would. But that's not the point. In a church as large as ours, it would be pretty hard to be available for all of those people, no matter how many pastors we had on our staff.

The lesson is clear. It is the church's job to equip *the people* to do the work of the ministry. I think I've heard that somewhere, haven't you?

THE A-B-C'S

Having a personal relationship with Christ is like having a relationship with anyone else. Knowing about Him is not the same as knowing Him personally. Sometimes God has to lead us down a painful path before we get to the point where we recognize our need for Him. That can be difficult but, once we arrive there, the next step of placing our faith in Jesus becomes very natural. Every weekend we close our services with this simple method to help people (1) to come to a saving faith in Christ and, (2) to reinforce for them how to lead members of their *oikos* to Christ when the occasion arises.

My staff and I preach to believers every weekend. We are fully aware that some, perhaps even many, in attendance are still pre-Christian, but we put our messages together assuming that everybody in that room is a Christian who wants to know how to better prepare themselves for the purpose of evangelizing their *oikos*. However, at the end of every message, we add this little challenge, "If you are with us today and you still have not come to know Christ personally, at High Desert Church we talk about the ABC's of coming to faith." Without short-selling the profound reality of spiritual regeneration, we try to present the components of salvation in a simple and transferable way.

A- **Admit** that you are a sinner who needs a Savior. Admitting our sin involves the Greek concept of confession. That's *homologeo* (Gr.), "to agree with." You have to agree with God that you're a sinner.

B- **Believe** that Jesus is the only Savior available. The Bible says that salvation is found in no one else. *No one else!* If you need a Savior from your sinfulness, you have only one choice, and that is Jesus, and only Jesus.

C- **Choose** to follow Christ, to accept Him into your heart. Repentance (*metanoia,* Gr.) requires that you make a conscious choice, actually change your mind about the way you're going to live your life; about putting Jesus on the throne of your life instead of yourself.

"Come follow me," Jesus said, "and I will make you fishers of men." The disciples had been fishers of fish and Jesus said, in effect, "I'm going to change the way you do life. Now we're going to go fishing for people's hearts."

And if you have not yet admitted your sinfulness, and you believe that Jesus is the only option for you to engage; if you want to take care of the sin problem in your life, be delivered from it's bondage; and if you have not yet chosen to cast your lot with Christ, then I would invite you to do that today.

That's exactly the same invitation to personally receive Christ that you would hear from me, encouraging people to follow the ABC's. It's simple. It works. In fact, if you attend our church for a year, you'll hear that simple Gospel presentation shared at least 52 times. The beauty of it is that people have learned how to share the Gospel without even intending to.

At some point it becomes so familiar to them that when that inevitable moment arrives and they're asked that question again, they simply respond, "Uumm, well, the Bible talks about A-B-C. The 'A' is for **A**dmit you're a sinner, and then **B**elieve that Jesus is the only Savior, and then make a **C**hoice to follow Him. Would you like to do that now? Let's pray together."

It just rolls up out of them, and it gives them the opportunity to kind of close the deal, if you will, on taking that step and placing their faith in Christ.

My first grade teachers, Mr. And Mrs. Cameron, a husband and wife team, added me to their oikos, and led me to Christ. They were always reaching out to my family and me and having me over to their house.

As an adult, God has used me to bring our two children to the Lord, as well as my brother. I have also invited people to church who gave their lives to Christ.

- Yvonne

Chapter Fifteen: HERE I STAND

You would think I'd be nervous. I even wondered if I'd be nervous, but when I came out on stage that Sunday morning, I wasn't. Here I was, about to introduce a whole new model for doing church to our people, and not even a nervous twitch. I'd had several discussions with my staff, small as it was at the time, and they were totally on board. But now I was standing on the end of the diving board, and we were all about to dive into the deep end. This wasn't just a four-kid youth group, this was my whole church. *Here we go*, I thought as I started to speak.

That was years ago, when High Desert Church was just a few hundred people. I should have been scared of the risk of introducing *oikos* as the entire heartbeat, purpose and model for our church, but it just seemed right. I can't totally explain it. The *oikos* model had become so indelibly imprinted on my thinking that when we took the step to make it everything, the hub of all we do and are as a church, it felt like a familiar groove.

I didn't know then how the Lord would use this model to grow His church, or how it would impact everything we would do. We learned fast that His vision was larger and more powerful than ours. We frequently had to run to catch up with what He was doing, and a big part of our challenge had to do with how we made decisions. Some time-honored things had to go because they didn't move the mission forward. We had to trust the Lord like never before because we had to surrender some of the control we were used to having by virtue of the many programs we had in place. Now it was up to the people and how they took the *oikos* model and implemented it in their lives.

DAVY CROCKETT WAS RIGHT

Davy had a motto, "Be sure you're right, then go ahead." That sort of sums up how I felt standing on that stage all those years ago. It just felt right, all the way down. So I went ahead. I presented the essence of what you've already read in this book, and over the next several weeks and months built on that until they understood it well enough to know if they wanted to be on board or not. I actually said, "We are going to be an oikocentric church, and if that's not what you want in a church, I know many good pastors and churches I can refer you to."

That didn't seem particularly bold to me at the time. I was just trying to clarify the situation for the folks. We had drawn a line in the sand. It was what some have called a "quality decision"—one about which you give yourself no further choice and from which there is no retreat.

What we didn't know at the time was all the rethinking we would have to do about the various elements of "doing church" that, up to then, we had taken for granted. We had to craft a whole new set of priorities and values based on the oikocentric model we had committed to. It took time and it has grown and matured as we have learned. And we're not finished yet.

DESIGN AND FUNCTION

As we developed this new model for how we would do church, we quickly realized that how we designed the structure of things would greatly influence how effective their functions would be. Design and function *are* connected, top to bottom. Our goal was to cooperate with how God designed us to function, because the design of anything reflects its value to the designer.

The church must train believers to live successfully. To live successfully as a Christ follower means to not only follow His teachings, but to do what He did—live an oikocentric life. Jesus poured His life into the Twelve, preparing them to change the world. In doing the Father's will, those men were Jesus' focus. But He didn't have long to get them ready. The deadline loomed larger as the Ascension drew closer. Jesus had to communicate to those men what the priority elements were that would frame the redemptive mission of the church. He had to cut to the chase, flesh out the core.

Jim Collins has written extensively about the importance of core values to any organization.[1] He describes how loosely we can use the term and attach it to components of an organization that aren't really core. He details that, in order for any value to be *core*, it has to be *essential*. Anything less couldn't be considered core. It has to be *enduring*. If it wouldn't last, what would be the point of building anything on it? It had to be *guiding*. A core value should be an indelible arrow, showing the way to greatness when more than one good option is available and tough decisions have to be made. And lastly, it had to be *non-compromisable*. That is, we would stick to it, even if the culture punished us for doing so.

Our first challenge, then, was to determine which core values would best enable us to support, teach and model this *oikos* lifestyle. Therefore, they must be the kind of values that would not only frame the ministry of our church but they must also become the core values for an individual's life, if pursuing worldchange were to be a life passion.

Here are what we have determined, for us, are those values.

TRUTHFUL

"Yet a time is coming and has now come when the true worshippers will worship the Father in spirit and truth, for they are the kind of worshipers the Father seeks." (John 4:23)

In a post-modern world, truth is defined by each individual and the community of which he or she is a part. That's why it seems as though nothing is certain anymore, that everything is evolving, changing and relative. Worldchangers see things differently. The Bible becomes their stripe clearly marking the centerline of life's road. It is, after all, the inspired, infallible and authoritative Word of God. It is not simply another tool among life's smorgasbord of self-improvement resources. We believe it is absolutely true. That is, it is true all the time, for everyone in every generation.

"For, 'All men are like grass, and all their glory is like the flowers of the field; the grass withers and the flowers fall, but the word of the Lord stands forever.' And this is the word that was preached to you." (1 Peter 1:24-25)

The Bible is the only document in the world that speaks with a divine authority and creates a divine empowerment that is unparalleled in any other literature. If you read it and still wonder if it is true, I say "Try it!" See if applying the principles it contains doesn't change your life from the inside out and make you the kind of person that you've futilely tried to be without it.

"All Scripture is God-breathed and is useful for teaching, rebuking, correcting and training in righteousness, so that the man of God may be thoroughly equipped for every good work." (2 Timothy 3:16-17)

The prophet Isaiah declared that everything else might fade away, but the Word of God will always prevail. More than anything else on Earth, what is written there is core. It is essential. It is enduring. It is guiding. And it is non-compromisable.

HELPFUL

You will find that virtually everyone in your *oikos* grew up attending church. Whether their background was Protestant or Roman Catholic, Mormon or otherwise, very few people will be entering a church for the first time when they come to yours! In fact, they were probably faithful attendees for years, having been taken by their parents on most weekends while they were growing up. But, that's the thing, they grew up! They weren't forced to attend any longer and so they stopped. Why? Because the church they grew up in didn't tell them truth? Perhaps, but not likely. At least I don't meet many people who say, "I grew up in church but stopped going because the pastor didn't teach the Bible." The reason they stopped attending was because church wasn't helpful.

As Christians, we need to help people connect the dots in their everyday lives between life experiences and God's love in a very real way. Even Christian disciplines become oikocentric. For example:

The discipline of Bible study—preparing to answer their questions, helping our *oikos* employ performance-enhancing principles to live by.

The discipline of prayer—acting as intercessors for our *oikos*, asking God to reveal His love to the people with whom we share life.

The discipline of generosity—reaching out to our *oikos* in the name of Jesus with His resources (none of it belongs to us anyway), letting God draw them to Himself through the kindness of His people.

The discipline of service--providing ministry systems that alleviate logistical obstacles that tend to discourage members of our *oikos* from attending church.

Every time I challenge believers to do anything in their Christian life, it is directly connected to their *oikos*. The high value of church is that it offers a place where believers actually become better prepared to be worldchangers, while we deepen our relationship with God by growing in each of those disciplines. In essence, church helps Christians learn how to be more helpful.

ENJOYABLE

Joy remains the most attractive quality on Earth. Cranky believers and boring churches are the best marketing tools for our enemy.

As the mother shook her young son back and forth, she told him in no uncertain terms, "Listen, we came to Disneyland to have fun and you're going to have fun whether you like it or not!" Well, I think that's a lot like many churches. People want to have a good time, but nobody really seems to know how. Religion (which is no fun) has replaced relationship (which is)!

Churches seem to be working harder all the time to make their worship services warm, inviting and enjoyable. But what happens after the service is over is what really matters. *Oikos* still remains the most effective arena for expressing the joy that Jesus provides.

"May the God of hope fill you with all joy and peace as you trust in him, so that you may overflow with hope by the power of the Holy Spirit." (Romans 15:13)

What overflows out of your life to the people around you? Do you find yourself feeling like a hypocrite, trying to offer hope but feeling hopeless? Wanting to help others but desperately needing help yourself? On the one hand, we're all in the same boat, offering our world a perfect Christ from a life context that is anything *but* perfect. But the privilege of sharing in the redemptive plan of God is pretty exciting, especially since He really *doesn't* need us anyway. That's the primary attribute of God—self-sufficiency. In other words, God will never need anyone or anything outside of Himself to accomplish His will.

When you think about it, it is a pretty lousy way to save the world. "Now, let me get this straight, Lord. You're going to come up with the genius of the Incarnation, make the effort of the cross, work the miracle of the Resurrection and then leave the Gospel in the hands of a group of reluctant, easily distracted followers?" Is that the best an omniscient God can come up with?

Evidently. And let me tell you why.

When my son was four, he asked if he could help me clean up the yard. I hesitated. I live in the desert. My yard was all I had to remind me that other colors beside shades of brown did exist, so it was a big deal to me. People would walk by and actually say that our yard looked like a park. And I'm supposed to partner with a four-year-old to keep it that way? I don't think so. But I looked in his bright eyes, saw the anticipation and couldn't resist the offer. A two-hour job ended up taking four, but what the heck? I was being offered the chance to spend quality time with Drew, share life and accomplish something beautiful together? Who could ask for more?

Jesus doesn't include us in the plan of evangelism because He needs us. I'm sure we actually double His workload, but He's hopelessly in love with us. He wants to spend quality time with us, share life with us and accomplish something beautiful together with us! And, in His mind, nothing is more beautiful than your world delivered.

DURABLE

For the past several years, our church has engaged a restructuring strategy that reflects our analysis of recent American church history. Most dynamic churches were born in this generation. Everywhere you look, virtually all of the great churches of former generations are merely a shadow of their glorious pasts. The few who are experiencing new life are doing so only after an extended season of decline, culminating in a combative, albeit, inevitable handover of power to a new generation of worshippers. Our conclusion, in short, is that there must be a better way to perpetuate the effectiveness of the local church.

For years, our challenge was to build an effective church. By God's grace, that happened. Now, our challenge is to build a durable one. After all, why should a generation pour millions of dollars of resources into campus development, minister efficiently to that single generation, gradually die out, and then leave a large facility to service an ever-decreasing congregation? In fact, as we see it, durability is the essential component that is missing from current church-planting strategies.

The same principle, though, is true for individual believers. Our strategies for personal growth should allow us the opportunity to pass life's finish line with the same joy and enthusiasm that we had when we first came into God's forever family. Likewise, those strategies should include doing whatever we can to perpetuate our spiritual legacy for generations to come.

That, then, is my desire for you, that you would employ the *oikos* principle, not just into your church but also into your life—asking God to reveal His Word to you; using you to help others find their groove in His Kingdom; so filling your heart with joy that it overflows to the people around you and keeping the excitement about the prospect of worldchange alive through your children and your grandchildren.

"My hairdresser and I exchanged phone numbers because we had a lot in common. A few months later, we were going to church together one night, and she and her husband accepted Christ at the end of the service."

- Myndi

"I'm a hairdresser, and one of my clients invited my husband and me to church. We were hesitant at first. My husband and I struggled with infertility for a few years and were running out of hope, so we decided we had nothing to lose. When we attended the young adult service, we wanted more.

We faithfully started coming to church and learning about God. About six months later, we found out we were going to have triplets! We gave our lives to God and have been blessed with three healthy sons. Now we can't wait to tell them what God has done in our lives."

- Lynsey

Chapter Sixteen: THE OIKOCENTRIC CHURCH

It is the job of Christ's church to prepare Christians for world-change. It's one thing to tell your people to "go get'em!" It's quite another to develop new ministry systems that will facilitate that process of preparation. If you want to be a part of an oikocentric church, the leadership of your church must consider the implications of that mission.

First, a pastor needs to determine how important *oikos* really is. The same thing is true with *oikos* as it is with every other aspect of your mission; leadership *has* to buy in. But I am telling you from experience, a pastor can't just make it an *oikos* evangelism program. It won't be successful, and then you'll blame me because it didn't work. *Oikos* has to permeate every discipleship element. It has to permeate every special event element. It has to permeate every worship service. It has to permeate every planning and strategy session you put together. It is everything. It's the only thing. It is the main thing!

I work with a mentoring group in San Diego about 150 miles south of where I live; we have a great time and we've developed a real bond. When the twelve of us started talking about *oikos*, I heard some say, "We have some key leaders we're going to have to convince, if we're ever going to make a commitment to an oikocentric ministry model."

So, we set up a small meeting where they could bring their leaders and I could share the *oikos* model with them. I remember one of the guys saying, "I shared it with one of the board members and he hated it, but he's coming to this meeting anyway as a favor to me." I reminded him of the necessity of his being fully persuaded first.

We had a couple of hours together at that meeting, and I think virtually all of them went away pretty excited about it. In fact, the one who was expected to be the most skeptical became one of the most vocal supporters in follow-up conversations. You must convince your key leaders of its import, no doubt. And if this book can help then I'm very glad of it.

Second, you have to commit to rethink every ministry system in your church. What that means in *your* church, only you know. I certainly don't pretend to know that. The core values you establish to support your restructuring strategies will be very important. They will naturally help you with your decisions about various programs and ministries.

Lastly, you cannot worry about over-emphasizing it. Every single week in every service our church hears about *oikos*. It is interwoven in the fabric of virtually every presentation we ever make. It's on everything we publish. We talk constantly about keeping the main thing the main thing. Just like with *oikos*, when we say, "The main thing in life is to keep the main thing…," and the entire congregation hollers back, "THE MAIN THING!" I mean, they know this. It's imprinted into the frontal lobes of their brains.

In our membership class, I tell all of the membership candidates, "If you are tired of hearing about *oikos*, you need to find another church, because I'm going to make you sick of it. But if you stay, it will ooze, it will bleed, and it will become part of your psyche."

YOUR WORLD DELIVERED

We can never be guilty of thinking so highly of ourselves that we start to think that our churches exist for us. The reason both your and our churches exist is for the people who don't attend them yet. But they will.

I say that because it is true. They will. And they're not just going to come to our church, they're going to come to yours. And they will come because, at some point, you began praying for them. By name, by need, you broke out your card and took every one of them to the throne of God every day, asking God to reveal Himself to them. You invited them to church, not just once but a gazillion times, and they always declined. But you kept praying. Every day. Each one.

And God began working in their lives, revealing Himself to them in a new way. You didn't even know it, but a need began to evolve in their family that actually exceeded their fears and broke down their resistance.

And then one day you asked those same friends again, "Hey, we're going to church Sunday morning, do you guys want to go with us and then go out to lunch afterward?" And they said, "Sure." You thought you didn't hear them right, because they had always said, "No, we've already got plans." So, trying your best to hide the shock on your face, you clarified, "You do?" And they said, "Yeah, it's time we went along to see why you guys love it so much!"

So you went, together. They weren't intimidated by the new environment because you were walking up the steps with them. You knew the ropes. You showed them where the kids were supposed to go. You introduced them to the childcare worker and even to the pastor.

And, then, the service was what you expected, what the service always is—truthful, helpful and enjoyable. The Bible was taught. Principles for life were clearly understood. The congregation was pretty fired up and joy permeated the entire campus.

All the way to the restaurant you were dying to ask them what they thought of the service, but you didn't want to come across too strong, so you waited. But later, as the Diet Cokes were being passed around, you couldn't stand it any longer, so you asked, "What did you think?" And they said, "It was different. It sure wasn't what we're used to, what church was like for us when we were growing up."

You talked about the funny story the pastor used to introduce his message and how the guitar player looked like the guy who worked at the grocery store, because he *was* the guy who worked at the grocery store. And that was it. You called it a day, a very good day.

The next morning, when their name was next on the list, you prayed differently. And the next time you asked them to join you, they readily accepted. And then again. And again. It was kind of funny to you, because they talked to your other friends like it was *their* church now! They were even inviting people to tag along. And then one night about three months later, at the same restaurant, one of them volunteered, "You know that prayer the pastor prays at the end of all the services, that A-B-C prayer?" You said, "Yeah?" They continued in a broken voice, "Well, I prayed with him tonight and invited Jesus to come into my life."

And as you watched, everyone around the table broke out in tears and hugs and high fives. Then you sank back in your seat—and it hit you! And you thought to yourself, "This is the reason I'm here. This is my purpose for being alive." You didn't say it. But you thought it, and for the very first time, you knew it.

It's the life you'd always wanted.

It's the deliverance your world had so desperately needed.

Oiko-homogeneity

If you're hanging out with a bunch of slobs,
then you have an...*oinkos*.

If you're touring with the Jonas Brothers,
then you have a...*boikos*.

If you're serving in the United States Navy,
then you have an...*ahoykos*.

If you're spending weekends at the lake with the same neighbors, then you have a...*toikos*.

If you're always having lunch with a group of vegetarians,
then you have a...*soikos*.

If you're spending a month with visiting relatives,
then you have an...*annoikos*.

If your group is working together to bring balance to The Force, then you have a...*droidkos*.

If you're hanging out with a group of fun-loving friends,
then you have an...*oiboikos*.

If you have a ministry in the Jewish community,
then you have an...*oive'kos*.

If you're shopping with friends who buy an awful lot of food and really big TVs, then you have an...*oikostco*.

End Notes

Chapter Two

1 Wolff, Hans Walter, Anthropology of the Old Testament, Mifflintown, PA: Sigler Press, 1996.

Chapter Three

1 Arn, Win, The Master's Plan, Pasadena, CA: Church Growth Press, 1982.

2 Reiner, Dr. Thom, "Ten Surprises About the Unchurched," Christianity Today, November 10, 2004.

3 Flugleman, Harry (Studio Chief at Goldsmith Studios), portrayed by Joe Mantegna in *The Three Amigos*, 1986.

Chapter Four

1 Kawasaki, Guy, Willow Magazine interview, Issue 3, 2007.

Chapter Five

1 Collins, Jim, Good to Great, New York, NY: Harper Collins Publishers, 2001.

2 Willard, Dallas, The Divine Conspiracy: Rediscovering Our Hidden Life in God, San Francisco, HarperCollins Publishers, 1998.

Chapter Six

1 Warren, Rick, The Purpose Driven Life, Michigan, Zondervan, 2002.

Chapter Eight

1 Richardson, Don, Eternity in Their Hearts, 1981.

Chapter Eleven

1 Aristotle, "Rhetoric Book 1, Written 350 B.C.," Translated by W. Rhys Roberts. Theology Website

Chapter Fifteen

1 Collins, Jim, and Porras, Jerry, Built to Last, New York, NY: Harper Collins Publishers, 1994.

Pastor Tom Mercer, the Senior Pastor of Victorville, California's High Desert Church has learned the power of the *oikos* phenomenon. After twenty-five years and leading a church from 150 to over 8,000 regular participants, he has also learned how to train people to understand it.

His messages are available online free of charge and, for a limited number of engagements per year, he is available to train your leaders or even challenge your entire congregation to consider their purpose for being here.

You can contact Tom through the High Desert Church website: www.highdesertchurch.com. You can find out more about *OIKOS, Your World Delivered* by watching a video in which Tom describes the need for *oikos* awareness, as well as order additional copies of this book at www.oikosbook.com. Orders of 10 or more receive a reduced price.